NO TURNING BACK

Jefe' Sails Solo, Non-Stop
Around the World

Jeffrey R. Hartjoy

No Turning Back:
Jefe' Sails Solo, Non-Stop Around the World

First Printing: 2018

ISBN: 978-0-692-17487-6

Visit our website:
www.sailorsrun.com

Dedication

To my soul-mate and loving wife Debbie, who was my much-needed sole land-based support team throughout this epic adventure.

To my family that struggled to understand the need for such great risks.

To all the people that rode along via email and kept me supplied with encouragement through some truly troubling times.

The Jefe'

To Zach

On our journey through life there are many adventures that are sure to pop up along the way. All we must do is summon the courage and passion to live them.

Jeffrey R. Hartjoy
"El Jefe'"

Thanks for being there for me in my time of need in Chamela, Mexico.

7¢ Each

Thanks for being there for me in my time of need in Obando, Mexico.

Contents

Introduction

"No Turning Back" is an amazing true-life sailing adventure, where the resourcefulness of a seasoned sailor is put to the test against all that nature can thrust upon him and his trusted war horse "Sailors Run".

In the beginning, a fast record-breaking trip was the goal, but from day one, it was obvious that nature and misfortune were to dictate a much different than expected outcome to the adventure. Not only was the Baba-40 "Sailors Run" continually degraded, but this veteran deep-water skipper, Jeff Hartjoy [the Jefe'¹], would be heaped upon by obstacles that had to be overcome to complete the voyage successfully. It becomes a battle for survival that threatens to reduce the skipper to a weakened soul, struggling to maintain his own sanity. With gear failure after failure, the duration of the voyage seems to keep extending. With many miles left to cover and food and water supplies rapidly depleting, the captain is forced to resort to extreme measures as he attempts to pull off his challenging quest.

Chapter 1: A Dream Emerges

Over the past 17 years, Debbie, my beloved wife of 31 years, and I have sailed over 85,000 nautical miles together, sharing our dream of traveling throughout the world, living among many different people and experiencing their unique cultures.

As one might expect, our appetites for such adventures would eventually differ, and one day, we would surely arrive at a point where a change in our cruising plans would dictate a new way to live out our dreams. I have always been a great advocate of compromise as being the means to keep the dream alive. Early on, it was just a matter of giving Debbie an opportunity to fly home to be with family for a month once a year. After nearly ten more years of cruising, the time period at home was extended to 2 months with family. Now, as you might imagine, this timeframe has been further extended and is now up to 6 months a year. This has allowed us to continue enjoying the cruising lifestyle, with Debbie joining me at times along the way and me being freed up to take on some truly great solo sailing adventures.

My first solo adventure was in 2008, when I sailed from Lima Peru around Cape Horn to Buenos Aires, Argentina. This challenging 5600 nautical mile adventure took 45 days of non-stop sailing, involving some wild ocean conditions. The entire story can be found in my book <u>Cape Horn, Ahead or Behind, Forever on My Mind</u>.

Now, some seven years later, the call for adventure has welled up inside of me, once again, and I feel obliged to take on the challenge of a solo circumnavigation via the southern five great capes[i]. At sixty-nine years of age, at last, I had a shot at realizing a lifelong dream of circumnavigating. It was also obvious that I wasn't getting any younger and could actually end up being the oldest American to have ever successfully accomplished this most challenging and dangerous feat.

I am truly fortunate that I have a wife that understands my love and passion for sailing and a family that grew up on boats, also well-aware of that same passion. I shudder somewhat just thinking of the immensity of such an undertaking, not to mention the preparation required if I hoped to have even the slightest chance at success.

It was time for me to look deep inside the sailor I have become and honestly evaluate whether I truly had the energy, tenacity, and will to pull this off. I also knew the risk for damage and cost of such a voyage would be placed solely upon Debbie and me, who are team "Sailors Run." Debbie and I kicked around the idea of sponsors, but in the end, I just didn't want to deal with the expectations and additional pressures put on us by such sponsorship. After all, if it isn't worth doing yourself, why get others involved?

I truly do not believe I would have undertaken a voyage such as this as a young man, as the possibility of a catastrophic failure with loss of one's life is a very real possibility. I knew this feeling would continually reside in the back of my mind for the duration of the voyage, and it would be necessary to keep it in check yet recognize it was there to keep me always on the alert. Deteriorating conditions would eventually put us at risk, and these would have to be dealt with quickly and in an orderly and professional manner.

A Dream Emerges
The vessel for the voyage.

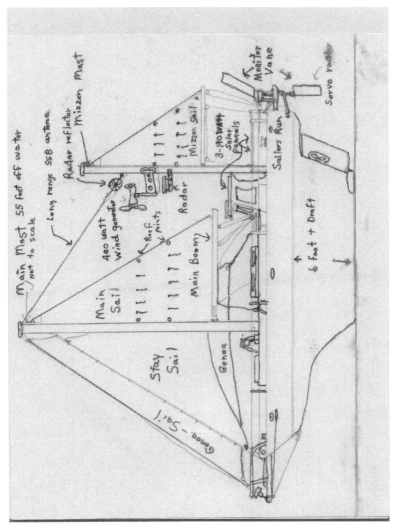

Chapter 2: Preparations

I have always been one to look far down the road, and it appeared that I had three years to accomplish the many preparations. Fortunately, our cruising plans would take us, once again, through the US, where many things that needed to be upgraded could easily be accomplished.

My biggest challenge was to formulate a financially viable plan that would ensure Sailors Run would be in top condition on the day of departure on this voyage. I tossed and turned many long and sleepless nights, trying to get a handle on all that must be done during this time.

I am not a wealthy person by any means. I quit my job as a line foreman for a power company and had not worked for the past 16 years. We have had to be very frugal, living off our investments and actually living on 800 dollars per month for a period of 5 years until I became eligible for social security. Knowing that time is the currency of life, Debbie and I have always valued a good quality of life over having things. We wanted to be able to spend our time freely, sailing about the planet, enjoying all that nature and the various cultures have to offer.

Once I had Debbie's support and she was on board with me in planning this adventure, we set sail from Bahía Caraquez, Ecuador.

Ecuador to Hawaii was no small feat, as we had to dance with Tropical Storm Rosa and the 60 knot winds and 20 ft. seas that were all part of it. Our arrival at the Big Island of Hawaii was the result of a fast 37-day passage covering the 5200 nautical miles at a good clip. We found ourselves enjoying paradise in the Hawaiian Islands with friends and spending many evenings making repair lists, as well as estimating costs to buy at least a few new sails. After all, we were now thousands of miles away from the actual starting line that

The Jefe'

was back in Bahía Caraquez, Ecuador, from where we had just come! I decided on Bahía as the starting place, knowing from there I could lay out a very fast route. Also, since you must enter the northern Hemisphere during your voyage, Bahía would be perfect, with the equator just 35 miles to the north.

After a great cruising experience in the islands over the 6-month cruising season, we were off to San Francisco. Departing from Hanalei Bay on the Island of Kauai, this was our second time to make this passage, and we were pleased with the outcome of this trip, reaching San Francisco in just 17 days, 5 days quicker than our last attempt on this route. We were able to sail all the way, skirting the Pacific high that had trapped us on the previous round, causing us to motor as much as we could with our eighty-gallon fuel supply.

Once in the San Francisco Bay Area, Debbie flew to be with her daughter and grandkids, while I hooked up with my son, Daniel. He had volunteered to sail up into the Delta with me, where we took on a very challenging project of building a new hard dodger for the upcoming voyage around the world. This took us three full weeks of steady work. We appreciated the wonderful atmosphere offered up in the "Delta." Thanks to my son, this project turned out to be a total success.

Once back down in the Bay Area at the marina, we set about replacing all the standing rigging on the main mast. With the mizzen rigging only 5 years old, it was deemed adequate for the upcoming tortures it would surely endure. I purchased many new lines, winch handles, flares, bilge pumps, and on and on. This was on top of all the other things that need to be upgraded as part of normal maintenance. Our final US stop for parts would be in San Diego prior to heading south in the 2013 "Baja Ha-ha".

As you might expect, the Baja Ha-ha, an 800-mile race, is lots of fun, and you end up in Cabo San Lucas after several days of generally great sailing. There are many fun-filled parties along the way, after which one tends to be ready to shift into a slower cruising mode! I felt much like I was marching in place, doing all these things along the way with the big adventure still a couple of years off; nonetheless, there were ongoing preparations to be made. I felt secure in the idea that there would be no big crunch before I took off—after all, I had plenty of time. Little did I know there were several things that were going to fly below the radar and escape my scrutiny.

At first, it seemed that only the mizzen sail would need to be replaced, but after a couple of small tears appeared in the main while tying it down on the boom, it became obvious that, after just 7 years, this sail was suffering from degradation from the sun. I knew the staysail would be called upon to keep us going in extreme conditions, and it was nearly new having seen very little use in the light airs of Mexico. The genoa was only 5 years old, and I had sailed around Cape Horn with our 10-year-old genoa previously with no problems, so I was confident this sail would endure the voyage.

My plan was to spend a year in Mexico before sailing south to Ecuador to get positioned for the start. I would wait to get there before returning home to say goodbye to family and friends. The new sails were ordered from Lee Sails, and I got the heavy 10.8 oz. material for durability. The sails would be flown back with me as part of my luggage, which was now becoming so great that I wondered, not only if they would let me on the plane, but also, if I would get all these final items through customs duty-free. It was a lingering worry! Debbie and I have had many challenges over the past 16 years trying to get boat parts back to the boat. In all honesty, it always seems to work out without any great expense, yet I always prepare for the worst and love being pleasantly surprised.

I spent the summer of 2014 in the Sea of Cortez in Mexico, a favorite haunt of Debbie and mine. This summer, however, turned out to be one with many hurricanes, and

The Jefe'

Odile, a category 4, nearly took out both the Sailors Run and me when I made a poor choice. I decided to try to weather it out as a tropical storm in a bay on the north end of the island *Isla de La Guardia*. I got caught short, as the storm moved very rapidly up the Baja Peninsula and then came across the Sea of Cortez, where I had anchored. Sailors Run had to weather out 85 knot gusts in an anchorage that eventually became exposed. Fortunately for us, we were anchored deep on tandem anchors that amazingly held, as our back was to the rocks. At one point, I had to prepare to abandon ship because, if the anchor had failed, there would only be a few minutes before we would be pulverized on the jagged rocks some 200 feet off our stern. This, by far, was the most frightening experience I have had and as close to losing my beloved "Sailors Run" as I have ever come. This exceptional experience had shaken my confidence and caused me to reconsider the need to try to circumnavigate solo—alone around the world nonstop. In the end, I still had lots of time to recover and ready myself before the kick-off day arrived.

Our gooseneck⸗ on the main boom had failed on the crossing from Hawaii to San Francisco and would be remanufactured in Mazatlán, Mexico. I stressed the need of a great design and repair to this most important piece of gear, and it appeared the new gooseneck was an adequate replacement.

Debbie and I cruised south along the Mexican Riviera all the way to the last port of Chiapas before leaving Mexico and, at that point, hauled the boat and applied new bottom paint. This meant it would be fresh and only 6 months old upon departure day for the circumnavigation.

Soon, Debbie and I set sail for Ecuador, a straight shot of several thousand miles to Bahía Caraquez. We escaped Mexico just ahead of the hurricane season and were in position for final preparations and provisioning. This would be accomplished over the next six months, and of course, there would be a quick trip back to the States to say goodbye to family and friends. Bahía Caraquez is a wonderful place where we have many friends that we met over the past eight years on our stop-overs. The boat is kept on a double mooring in the Rio Chone River, and the Puerto Amistad Restaurant is a great place to hang out with friends and sip on a cold beer while you gaze out upon your boat resting on the moorings.

It was early May, and it wouldn't be until late October that I would depart Bahía Caraquez on the circumnavigation. This meant I would have to get a 6-month visa that cost about $400, in addition to the $180 I had already paid for our 3-month visa. It is continually getting more expensive to check in and out of most countries by boat, something that seems truly unfair compared to most tourists that do it for less than $30 when traveling by air. I feel the true sense of freedom is under attack, and governments are doing what they can to discourage this form of travel in an attempt to keep you at home to spend your money in your home country. It is this encroachment on the freedom of the sea that makes it more and more attractive to me. Until you become one with nature, you will never truly grasp this concept and the rush of freedom that comes from being self-reliant and free from government bureaucracies.

Debbie got me settled in the Bahía routine, and after about a month, she flew out to be with her family in Albuquerque. I stayed behind, working on the boat, refinishing the brightwork", and installing additional safety items, such as an automatic bilge pump and high-water alarm. I also installed an A.I.S." collision avoidance system that would let me know where ships were, including their course and speed, and transmit a signal letting them know I'm under sail with my course and speed. This safety feature is a tremendous asset for the solo sailor, especially way off shore, where, most likely, traffic will be large vessels that also have A.I.S. I also installed

The Jefe'

an enhanced alarm to be sure I could hear it even if I am sound asleep.

The house we built and sold to afford to live our dream aboard Sailors Run.

Sailors Run in Chiapas Mexico sporting new dodger, solar panels, and bottom paint.

New chain plates being installed for split backstay.

Baggy wrinkle under construction to help prevent chafe on such a long passage.

The equipment needed to get aloft when sailing single-handed aboard Sailors Run.

New mainsail hoisted in Bahia Caraquez.

Chafe gear being applied to sharp back edge on spreaders.

Chapter 3: Back Home for Final Goodbyes

I departed Bahía for the U.S. with a bit of a lump in my throat, as I was leaving my vessel and means to sail around the world unattended on a mooring in the river mouth of the Rio Chone. I could only hope and pray the marina security would be adequate to keep "Sailors Run" safe. There was some reason for concern as, recently, several boats had been robbed while the owners were away, and I could only hope that our networking with the local people would help ensure the boat's safety in my absence.

I flew first to New Mexico to catch up with Debbie, our son Chris and his family, as well as many of Debbie's relatives. This trip was also designed, not only to give me one last shot at getting needed things for the voyage, but also to promote my first book, Cape Horn. Debbie, being my promoter, arranged a book signing at Hastings Books and set up a presentation for later in the summer in San Francisco at the Corinthian Yacht Club. I must admit that public speaking has never come easy for me, but I was amazed how easy it is when you are talking about what you know about and are sharing something for which you truly have a passion.

New Mexico has an arid climate that my older bones and joints seem to enjoy. Both Debbie and I enjoy getting out and running or walking on a regular basis, as this is our medical insurance, and it keeps us fit for the active lifestyle that we have chosen for ourselves. The 5,000-foot elevation does tend to tax our lungs until we become accustomed to it.

I have always enjoyed writing and being able to share the adventures that we have embarked on with others. I try to make the reader feel they are there with us as we venture forth into uncertainty and sometimes danger.

The Jefe'

After a month in Albuquerque, it was time to head northwest. This trip was truly going to be different, as we decided to take the Amtrak where possible, and that meant going to Colorado first. Our son drove us partway, then our friends, John and Dee, came down to pick us up and take us to their place for a few days' visit. They live in Pagosa Springs, Colorado, where they have a restaurant and a couple of homes. John and Dee are two great friends that we met while sailing in Mexico; they were down there at the same time on a vacation and had rented a house with a pool on the beach.

I must share with you that my wife, Debbie, meets everyone, and somehow, we always get hooked up with nice people in faraway places. After five wonderful fun-filled days exploring a part of Colorado that we had never seen, it was time to hop the Amtrak to San Francisco. There, we would meet up with my son, Daniel, who lives there with his girlfriend, her daughter, as well as my two granddaughters. Once we caught the Amtrak in Junction City, Colorado, we settled in for the two-day trip to San Francisco. I was just hoping I would not end up barfing all over the train, as it had been years since I had ridden the rails. As it turns out, I was fine, as was Debbie, but I became well-aware of how degraded our railroads in the US have become. The trains are slow, much slower than going by car, yet very comfortable, which helps to make up for the slow mode of travel. The conductors on the train are big guys, as they need to be to maintain order with, at times, a somewhat suspect clientele riding the rails. The train has rules, and they must be adhered to or there would be chaos on board, which we nearly had on several occasions during our trip.

Once at my son's, I was able to pick up a few boat parts I needed from the Bay Area. Of course, there is never enough money or room to carry all that you might need for circumnavigation! We stayed first with my son Dan and Anna, hanging out with them and the three girls. My son and his girls have lived aboard since the girls were born, and they are very comfortable around the marine environment. Daniel has two boats, a 45-foot sailboat and a 56-foot power boat on which he, Anna, and the girls live. Our good friends, Bruce and Pascale, have a home in Tiburon, and it was their yacht club where I did a slide show about "Living the Dream." The opportunity to do two more shows evolved from that speaking engagement, so I guess I did OK.

Time was flying, and we had to get up to Washington State, where my other son and daughter live, not to mention my sister Bonnie, with whom I have always been close. The train ride north was much shorter, and the scenery along the way was equally beautiful as the previous trip through the Rocky Mountains. There was something different in the good-byes this time, different than when I made my trip around Cape Horn in 2008. Now, with a much more dangerous voyage ahead, friends and family had come to know me well enough to understand that, not only was I capable of such a voyage, but that there would be little chance to turn me from it. Instead, they gave encouragement and support in the place of doubt and skepticism about such an undertaking. I also felt much different. Realizing the magnitude of such an undertaking was so big that I could hardly get my head around it and had some uncertainties about how I really felt about it. It was almost like there was this thick fog between me, my planning, and what I was really getting myself into. This was something I wouldn't come to grips with until crossing the finish line back in Bahía.

I picked up the mainsail and mizzen that had been delivered to my sister's address and knew these were two of the final items necessary to fill out my punch list of necessary new equipment. You know, when you work towards getting everything right for the trip and you start adding up the costs, it doesn't take long to start rationalizing why you can get by without certain upgrades or replacements. It seemed to me that maybe I was doing too much and spending too much. This was proven to be a very false line of thinking. I believe I struggled with it because I really didn't fully comprehend the effects of the extreme conditions that I would be sailing in for so many months on end.

After two months with family and friends, it was time for Debbie and me to say our final goodbyes, then I climbed aboard a jet and headed back to the boat in Ecuador. I was amazed at how smooth things went going back through customs in Ecuador. They seemed to have little interest in all the bags of gear I was bringing into the country. The local bus drivers seemed to think I was packing too much stuff along with me, and they didn't want to load it under the bus I was taking back to Bahía. I paid them an extra five dollars, then all was well, and we were on our way. When the cab dropped me at the Puerto Amistad marina, I was nearly back to the boat. My mind couldn't help but say a silent prayer that I would climb aboard the boat and find it locked up tight and secure.

Pedro, the security guard, motored me out to Sailors Run, and she looked great as we approached, resting peacefully on her moorings. I climbed on board, asking Pedro to hang on for just a minute while I had a look below to see if there was any sign of forced entry. All appeared to be just as I had left it. I went back topside and tipped Pedro twenty dollars and thanked him for keeping the boat safe during the more than two months I had been away.

Chapter 4: Provisioning

With still nearly two months before departure day, I knew I would be busy all the way to the end. I replaced the bearings on the main shaft in the wind generator and was pleased with myself that I could do it from the bosun's chair while up the mast. Not having to take down the generator was a major benefit. I sanded and put the final coat of paint on all the brightwork, making sure we had maximum protection on the wood. I ascended both masts to do a final rigging inspection and re-do the boots on the spreaders. I also added additional chafe gear on the spreaders that, otherwise, are a little too sharp for the new sails to be rubbing on for months on end.

I started making frequent trips to the local stores, all the time trying to find the best prices on canned goods. Unfortunately, most people in Ecuador shop every day for their dinner that night and eat fresh vegetables from the market. This seems to make for limited supplies of canned goods, especially when it comes to variety and good sale pricing. When I returned to the boat, I was always amazed with what seemed like a virtual mountain of supplies and the way they just seemed to disappear into the massive storage areas that this "Baba" sailboat has!

Soon, I was down to my final two weeks in port, and there were a few time-sensitive things that had to be done. One of these items was to get the weight out of the bow of the boat. I removed and stowed the chain from the bow to amidships, as well as buried the primary 60-pound CQR anchor in an aft compartment where it could be secured for the wild ride that lay ahead. Our secondary anchor would be left with our friends, Dave and Judy, up at Saiananda, where they are building a new home. They were most helpful, allowing us to store our outboard motor and dinghy there, along with the forward

The Jefe'

and aft cabin doors, as these are very heavy and rarely closed so of no use on this trip.

The boat was sitting lower and lower in the water every day, as we were provisioned for 6 months-plus, and would be carrying 160 gallons of water, 80 gallons of diesel, along with 22 gallons of gasoline for the Honda generator. The diesel would only be used to run the motor for fifteen minutes once a week to circulate the oil and keep the moisture out of the engine, not for propulsion. The gasoline most likely would not be used and only if all other means of charging failed to keep up with our electrical needs. The three 140-watt solar panels go a long way towards doing this, and with the 400-watt wind generator, I felt in pretty good shape. One thing that worried me was having enough propane with which to cook. I already had two 5-gallon bottles and picked up a spare 5-gallon bottle in Mexico on our way down. The only problem with the Mexican bottle is that it has no screw to vent the bottle while filling. When gravity feeding to fill them, as they do here at Puerto Amistad, it takes days to get that bottle filled, and only my friend Dave was able to get it anywhere near full.

The last thing I did was dive the bottom and was very pleased with how well the bottom paint was holding up, now six months old and still no signs of growth except a little at the waterline. I coated the prop with Desitin ointment, a wonderful way to keep things from growing on your prop.

I purchased six pounds of peanut butter at the market for two dollars a pound then added oil and sugar to it, mixing it in the blender and storing it in three plastic one-quart jars. I must admit it seemed to me that I was truly going overboard on this provisioning, and surely, there was no way I could possibly eat all of this stuff. I mean there was hardly a spare inch of storage space left anywhere with all lockers and bilges being "chock-a-block" full!

Provisioning

Our friends John and Dee flew in from Colorado to visit Bahía and see me off. I put in for my international *zarpe*", and there was some confusion. How could I get a *zarpe* to come right back to the same country without first stopping somewhere along the way? In the end, they just put down the Marquesas as my next port of call, as they had no way to do what was actually going to happen. But they assured me that, since I was returning in a different year, it could all work out. I had no dinghy and had to rely on other cruisers and the security guard to get back and forth to the boat.

Finally, my last day in Bahía had arrived. I spent time with Dee and John and bid farewell to the staff at Puerto Amistad, a wonderful bunch of people. With my paperwork in hand, I was taken back to the boat about 3 p.m. to make final preparations for the 5 a.m. departure. I crawled into my sea berth that was made up behind the lee cloth at about 9 p.m., and although anxious about the early morning departure, I managed to slip into that final night of undisturbed sleep.

Provisions include ingredients for splicing the "Main Brace".

You never know when beer and chips might be in order.

Drying out cabbage and potatoes; note spot locator on the rail.

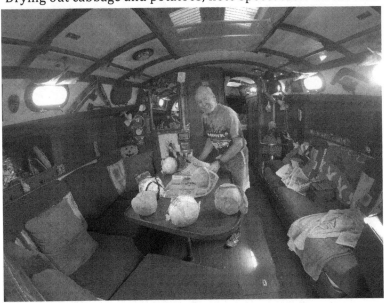

Dry cabbage wrapped in newspaper will last about two months.

Another Harvest from the store.

It was obvious nothing more was going in the refrigerator.

The bilge was home to many of the heavier provisions.

Surely, it will be impossible to eat all this stuff.

There is food everywhere and, of course, lots of cookies.

Provisioning

There was no shortage of safety gear aboard Sailors Run.

My mini weather station.

Chapter 5: The First 30-Days

120°W   110°W   100°W   90°W   DAY-4   DAY #1
Take evasive action to avoid...
Fishing Boat

Equator
0°

Galapagos Islands

DAY-5   Short Spin
Discover Fuel Tear in Genoa.
culador

DAY-1
Crossed Equator for 12th & 13th times. Also Wind Generator Fails.

PERU

10°S

DAY-11

20°S   DAY-13
Discovered mal functioning automatic Bilge pump

DAY-15
While running main in nuetral, free wheeling prop
Vibrates Nut off prop shaft and prop few wheels in to rudder.

DAY-18   Easter Island
30°S   Abeam off

DAY-20

Day-21
Went up mast to repair Wind generator
No luck its done.

DAY-25

DAY-24
Caught 15lb.
Big Eye Tuna

First 30 DAYS of Voyage
3968 nm. Sailed So far.

40°S

DAY-30
Nailed by first Big Storm

45°S

First - 30 - DAYS

DAY 1

The alarm was blaring in my ear, and at last, 4 a.m. had rolled around. I crawled from my berth, shutting off the alarm. Now, with just an hour to go before the pilot showed up, I got the coffee going and had a quick bowl of cereal, knowing the next few hours would be hectic getting out to the start. Up on deck, I attached the sail halyards to the two sails that had been uncovered the night before and were ready to be hoisted. I was down below, getting the computer set up to show the starting line on the electronic chart, with the GPS showing the position of Sailors Run before the start. Suddenly, I heard a thump on deck as the pilot crawled aboard. I went topside and started the motor. We were to follow the pilot boat out the pass once he had retrieved our official starter, Tripp Martin, the present owner of Puerto Amistad. Within minutes, we were free of the mooring, starting a slow passage out from the river mouth towards the pass and out over the bar. Tripp, now in the Panga[vii], came aboard to ride out through the pass with us. All went well on the way out, and soon, I released the pilot, and Tripp went with him back into the panga, where they filmed me getting under sail and heading to the start.

The date was October 31, 2015 and Halloween. A few people lined the shore to see me off, and of course, our good friends Dee and John were there, watching as I got underway. I crossed the starting line at 7:09 a.m. Bahía Caraquez, Ecuador time. The wind was coming in on the beam, making fast work of reaching the Equator, our 12th crossing of it. After going a mile into the northern hemisphere, I immediately came about on the opposite tack, having toasted King Neptune twice as we crossed back into the southern hemisphere on our 13th crossing. The winds were piping up, and we were shooting south close inshore until we neared Bahía once again. Around dusk, the winds shifted to the south, and I tacked over onto the port tack, heading off-shore towards the Galapagos Islands some 500 nautical miles to the west.

Tonight would require staying out in the cockpit with the radar on, looking out for small fishing vessels while only taking short 15-minute catnaps. I can assure you, although this might work short term, it is no good long term, day after day, because your body needs some deep sleep, and that means staying down for at least 2+ hours at a time. I must admit I was getting more than just a little concerned that there appeared to be a problem with the wind generator. It had been braking throughout the day, coming to a stop then taking off again, only to brake and stop, once again, all the time producing no power. I was hoping this could be rectified by checking all the wiring connections between the base of the mizzenmast and the batteries. On my previous Cape Horn Trip, the wind generator had kept up with my power needs for the entire trip.

DAYS 2-4

The next three days were spent adjusting to life at sea. I had to become accustomed to the constant motion and had to become one with both Sailors Run and the ocean, which would become my way of life for the next five to seven months. It seems, when ocean voyaging, one is seldom fortunate enough to sail the rhumb line course, the shortest distance, thereby taking the shortest route to your desired destination or turning point. We were making good speed and about 30 degrees off course, sailing just about as close to the wind as possible, yet maintaining maximum speed on a close reach, a fast point of sail for Sailors Run.

DAY 5

The days were sunny and warm, in the eighties and only cooling off slightly at night, making for ideal sailing conditions. We reached the SE-trades at last and were able to sail the desired course more to the southwest. The Galapagos Islands are just 150 nautical miles away, and for some time, I had been wondering if we were going to be able to get south of them. The wind began to strengthen, and it was necessary to roll in the genoa to reduce its size and ease some strain on the rig, thereby reducing heel and rudder drag caused by the weather helm that the excessive heel was causing. I clipped in and went forward as we bashed along at a brisk clip in 15-18 knots of breeze. When I got up on the foredeck and was checking the current sheeting angle, I suddenly felt another pang of anxiety, as I was staring at a six-inch tear in the genoa. Here we are, just starting into the voyage, and this is the second thing that appears to be wrong! I quickly roll in the genoa further, burying the tear into the rolled-up sail. The repair will have to happen when the winds have abated and I dare let out the sail. It looks like I can patch the sail on the fly, thereby not having to pull the whole thing down on deck and out of the foil.

I go below and prepare dinner, a small fried chicken breast and a salad made from a variety of fresh vegetables. I like to eat just two meals a day when at sea and cap it off with tea and a cookie for dessert. I am amazed at how well-adapted I have become to reading on my Kindle and its amazing ability to store so much literature in such a small place.

It was late in the afternoon when we sailed close by a commercial fishing vessel with three small sailing launches in tow. The fishing in the waters off the Galapagos Islands is obviously very good in these nutritionally rich waters brought all the way up from Antarctica by the Humboldt Current. That also makes the water much cooler than the local air temperature. Seeing this vessel was proof enough that tonight would require a near constant vigil. It was about one in the morning when I first sighted a large white glow emanating over the distant horizon. This glow seemed to stay close off the port bow, and there was going to be no going back to sleep, as it was now definitely getting closer. After one and a half hours with the wind vane continually altering our course back and forth about ten degrees, I was amazed that we maintained on this collision course. The vessel, though highly visible and far out to sea, was transmitting no A.I.S. signal identifying itself, and since we were in Ecuadorian waters not so far from the Galapagos Islands, most likely, this had to be an Ecuadorian boat. Now within two miles, it was time to resort to evasive action, and I tacked back to the north, sailing clear of what might have been an impending collision, all the time not too happy that, on this huge ocean, we had to come to this. Oh well, it was only fifteen minutes, and I felt confident in tacking back onto the desired course, and within the hour, the fishing boat's lights were only a faint glow over the horizon. I slipped off into a wonderful deep sleep for several hours before the sun popped up over the eastern horizon, shining brilliantly into a crystal-clear sky above an ocean that was rapidly turning a deep cobalt blue.

DAY 6

Wow, we're hauling ass, slamming along to weather as I try to put together a bowl of cereal—which should be easy you would think—but guess again. First, I get a cup and go forward, bouncing about on my way, and open the hanging locker that has some shelves in it that hold the powdered Lido milk. I pop the lid off the can and somehow manage to get most of the three spoons full of powder into the cup, and the rest settles as a white dust on the door jamb. Now, it's a dance back to the galley sink and countertop, where I set the cup and retrieve the cold water from the fridge and mix a cup of milk that I pour over my favorite granola cereal. Now, I like to soak that granola awhile to soften it up a little. The cereal bowl wants to slop its contents all over the galley, and I'm forced to put the bowl on a burner of the gimballed stove, where I clamp it down with the metal fiddles that normally would hold a pan in place. At last, I'm free to get the canned fruit out of the fridge to add to the already quite large bowl of cereal, and now, I can eat my breakfast. I really have no need to work out to stay in shape, as I'm doing dynamic tension exercises all day just hanging on and anticipating the next big move. If it's not that, it's grinding in sails with the winches out on deck.

We have been averaging about 150 miles a day, and I'm pretty pumped up, feeling that this truly could be a record non-stop run for a solo sailor of my age, 69 years.

DAY 7

I took a reef in the main this morning as we were a little over-powered, and it made life aboard so much more comfortable. Now, both main and mizzen are reefed. The genoa is in about 20% to keep the tear rolled in to avoid making it larger. The staysail is full on, at 100%, and we are sailing great. There are more flying fish and squid on deck this morning. They would surely make fine bait, but the freezer is still too full to fish.

I got an email from a friend, and he says "f**k" the wind generator as he knows of a power company that invested in them and nearly bankrupted the utility. The sad part of that was the people on the system that had nearly the cheapest rates in the nation before the free wind power, now watched their rates double in just a couple of years and struggle under huge debt. Having said that, I truly miss mine and hope to get it going again. Each morning, I use about a quart of water rinsing off the three solar panels with a sponge as the salt spray reduces their effectiveness.

Even at 80°F, I'm noticing the cooling below deck as we move further south, and the moisture in the air is starting to make things feel cool and damp.

DAY 8

With squalls in the area, a sailor needs to be a bit more cautious. I normally reef down a little more at night and mentally go through the drill in my mind as to how I can get all sails down and in what order, as it can be very *chaotic* if overtaken by a severe squall at night while asleep. Radar is your first line of defense because the size and distance they are from you can be measured and tracked. Typically, the power of the wind in a squall is determined by the size. My experience is that anything two miles or less in size seldom requires reducing sail. With the small ones, you can just sail off downwind until they pass over, which is normally no more than twenty minutes. A squall that is two to four miles across can be more serious, especially if you are already sailing hard, as the wind strength will most likely double for twenty to thirty minutes as it goes over you. When the squall is six to eight plus miles across, it is time to get serious about reducing sail, especially if you are already sailing hard and fast. I know of several boats that were caught in large line squalls such as this and had all their sails destroyed as they failed to get them down in time and watched them blow out in winds in excess of 60 knots. Once again, radar gives you the ability to know the size and distance, night or day.

DAY 9

Current Stats

Position
Lat. 10°54'S / Long. 96°07'W

Weather
Barometer = 1010 mb. -- Wind = 8-18 kts. - - Temp = 73°-78°

Seas
4-6 ft.

Distance
24 hr. run = 150 NM
Miles sailed last three days = 458 NM
Total miles sailed so far = 1266 NM
Miles left to go to turning point for the Horn = 1952 NM

Top speed so far
9.8 kts.

This morning when I awoke, things were quiet aboard, and we had slowed to just over four knots. I knew now was my chance to roll out the genoa and patch the sail. While bouncing around clipped into the bow pulpit, I applied sail tape to both sides of the tear that was about six inches long and one layer of sail material glued down with contact cement before getting it rolled back up on the furler^{viii}, as the wind had piped back up. Repair on the fly to be continued. Several hours later, there was another lull in the wind strength, so I eased out the sail just enough to get at the tear. I did a little dance on the bow platform, juggling the can of contact cement and my chisel as I applied the cement and eventually secured the second piece of five-ounce sail material to the other side. Then the real fun began, sewing the patches together on a plunging bow, possibly much like doing needlepoint on a pogo stick. After about one hour, the patch was complete, and Sailors Run was ready to go with a genoa that could be rolled all the way out, "yahoo!"

Later, I noticed a peculiar odor coming from the vegetable storage area. It smelled much like a rabbit hutch I once had, or maybe it was that Guinea pig cage I kept in my bedroom as a child. I suspected that my six cabbages wrapped in newspaper need to be trimmed down and re-wrapped.

Today is shower day, as I take one every three days whether I need it or not, and trust me, I'm doing the right thing!

DAY 10

Wow, this is a fabulous sailing day. With 15-25 knots, we are moving fast and surrounded by dolphins frolicking off our bow waves. I grab the GoPro camera and film away. I truly love the fact that I do not have to worry about getting it wet as we bash along with spray flying. I have three cameras along for the trip and learned from taking video on my last truly great adventure, the trip around Cape Horn, that I have to cut way back on the all-nude shots!

After re-wrapping the cabbages, it was time to take my once-every-three-day shower. A shower at sea when sailing close to the wind with a good-sized sea running is truly an event. I get by with just three quarts of water in a bowl that can hold that much and still have enough empty bowl left to keep the water from slopping over the sides. I then use a small cup to get me totally wet while hanging on in the shower stall or sit on the seating in there. Once wet, I wash my hair with shampoo and soap up every place else then use the cup and remaining water in the bowl to rinse off. When I got out and was toweling off, the boat rolled hard to one side, and I was forced to lean my backside into the keel stepped mast that resides there in the head area. Well now, that is definitely a cold-ass experience!

Once clean, I figured it was time to wash some of the laundry that was accumulating in my small hamper; after all, this warm weather and sunshine will gradually go away. I tied up some clotheslines behind the hard dodger where they were protected and soon had them all covered with fresh wet laundry. All was well and good until being overtaken by a squall, and the laundry received a second rinse. During this squall, I had to roll in the genoa about 40%, and all the time I was cranking on the winches, I was getting the crap slapped out of me by the flapping laundry that was flailing wildly. By the end of the day, the laundry was dry and smelt fresh and clean.

All and all, this was to be a great day, logging 176 nautical miles along our course line. With days like this, I was getting optimistic that, just possibly, I might come close to Dodge Morgan's record solo run around the world of 150 days, and of course, that was on a 60-foot specially-built boat for such a trip. Well, at least I could hope and dream.

DAY 11

Now, more than 1200 miles off the coast of South America and just a little south of Lima, Peru, I sight my first ship since the encounter with the fishing vessel. This vessel is a large ship, and thanks to A.I.S., we are aware it is there by a signal received from the ship. It never got closer than 31 miles. I realize, since I'm this far out to sea, any major problems that occur become much more significant, and we are getting further from help every day.

We are skirting the west side of the South Pacific high, heading for the west side of Easter Island and on to the roaring forties where we hope to pick up the westerlies that will kick us on around the planet.

DAYS 12-13

I find the temperatures dropping, and it might be time to eat beans and pop open some more beer cans in hopes that the CO_2 will drive the global warming and temperatures up a little, at least below decks.

The First 30-Days

It was during the night that I awoke to the sound of a motor running. I struggled to get out of my berth and from the cozy confines of the lee cloth. I staggered past the radar, glancing at it to see that the screen was still clear, then ascended the stairs and knocked the companionway doors open with a bang. Once in the cockpit, I gazed into the coal black darkness, looking for lights and listening for the motor sound, but there was nothing to be heard but the sloshing of the sea as Sailors Run sailed through it. Once back below, I listened again yet still nothing heard. Settling in my berth, I could hear the motor start up, and it was obviously cycling on and off. Up again, I opened the door under the sink to see if this was, in fact, coming from the refrigeration. No, that was not it, as it was much quieter and was just purring along. I sat down on my bunk, wondering what in the hell could this be. Once again, it started, and suddenly, it dawned on me. Turned out, it was the new automatic bilge pump I had installed cycling on and off.

I pulled up the floor boards, and there was a small amount of water splashing around the automated pump. This was a problem, because the high dollar pump that might work great at anchor was surely going to drive me nuts if I didn't pull the fuse on it. Now, I would have to inspect this particular area every once in a while. I have a high-water alarm that would sound if the water did rise to that level. The water in there now was about one quart, and I had no real worry about it. It was under my aluminum fuel tanks, and I had fiber-glassed across the bottom and half way up the sides as a safety measure should I get some water in that part of the bilge.

DAY 14

After two weeks at sea, I have eaten many of the fresh vegetables I had stowed aboard. I still have some tomatoes and, of course, lots of cabbage, onions, potatoes, and a couple of large squash. I still have a few oranges and thirty apples. I'm sure you have heard of the cannibals from years ago that populate many of the Pacific Islands. Well, I too will soon become a cannibal, as just about everything I will eat will come from a can. It really isn't so very different from being a vegetarian. The only slight difference is the canatarian needs a can-opener, and that's about it. Putting out a fishing line is starting to look like a good idea, as there seems to be some room in the freezer now.

After two weeks, I'm still on my first tank of 75 gallons of water. Once we suck that tank dry, it will be time to fire up the Pur 160 water maker.

The past two weeks have been some of the best sailing I have yet to experience, and we are covering a lot of ocean fast. I have been pulling faxes and GRIB files daily to stay on top of the weather and help make sure I make it around safely.

DAY 15 - CHANGE IS IN THE AIR

I imagined myself being sling-shot around the bottom of the South Pacific high, making great time to the roaring forties, but the weather at times can do whatever it wants. A second high has formed directly ahead along my intended course, and my sailing speed is slowing down. As I check the weather far to the south in those roaring forties, it is kicking up forty knots of wind and thirty-foot seas, with zero visibility and lots of rain. Hmmm, that looks inviting.

My previous book _"Cape Horn," Ahead or Behind Forever on Your Mind_, definitely was in my mind as we continued to venture deeper into the Southern Ocean.

Today, it was time to run the engine in neutral to circulate the oil, warming the motor a little and drying it out for about 15 minutes. I went topside, shutting off the motor, and popped the transmission back into reverse, thereby locking the propeller, as after all, a boat sails faster with the prop not spinning. Once down below, I could feel a strange vibration through my feet, and it seemed the shaft was turning. I hurried out into the cockpit and pulled everything out of the portside compartment, so I could gain access to the transmission and drive line. Once down in there, I was shocked at what I was seeing. The shaft was wildly spinning and wobbling as it had pulled free of the hub that connects it to the transmission. The only thing stopping the shaft from exiting the boat was the rudder, and the three-blade prop was spinning wildly out of control and chewing away at it. I grabbed a piece of ½" line and tied one end to some framework then carefully worked five wraps onto the rapidly spinning shaft that was wobbling. I pulled as hard as I could to cinch the line on the shaft, and gradually, it began to slow down. We were sailing at good speed, so there was a lot of pressure on the prop, trying to tear it loose from the grip of the line. I secured the other end of the line to a cross member and started pulling the shaft forward to bring it clear of the rudder. The only problem with this was that now a steady stream of water began to flow in around the shaft at the damaged packing gland. Holy shit—what next?!

Now, it was time to slow down the boat, so I could take some pressure off the prop and shaft that was trying to start turning again. With the headsail rolled in and the staysail down, I hove-to* under main and mizzen sails, making the shaft much easier to control. I knew what had happened. Somehow, the nut on the shaft had vibrated off, and the shaft slid out. Unfortunately, the shaft key had disappeared into the depths of the bilge that was now flooding, forcing me to climb out of the confined space and go turn on the bilge pump every five minutes. Fortunately, I have a powerful extendable magnet onboard for fishing things from the bilge. I could not believe my good fortune as I came up with the key on my first attempt, and it appeared to be in good shape. The other two parts, the lock washer and nut, were trapped in the connecting hub that was still bolted onto the transmission. I unbolted the hub and had the nut and washer ready to go back on. Once the key was in place, the hub slid down over it. There was nothing

I could do about the flood of water coming from the packing gland until the shaft was bolted back on to the transmission. I had to make many trips up to turn on the bilge pump, all the time trying to get the hub back up on the transmission. Even though we were sailing slowly, it was difficult to control the shaft. I bolted the hub on but was shocked to find that I did not have the proper socket to tighten the nut properly. I tightened it as much as I could by hand then used a socket that was just a little too big to get some torque on it. Since I only needed this motor to avoid collision and get in the river back to Bahía, I was not too concerned about the tightness, although the prop would be freewheeling when I ran the motor in neutral every two weeks.

Now came the hard part, untying the shaft so I could pull the shaft with the coupler bolted on, up against the transmission flange. Then I had to get that first bolt through the hole, while trying to keep the shaft from turning and pulled up tight in place long enough to get a nut started on the other end. I struggled and pulled like a Missouri mule, getting the shaft in place, and after no less than a dozen tries and about twenty minutes later, at last, I got that first bolt in place and partially tightened. The water level had risen very high in the bilge as I had to let it flood until I finally had the bolt in place before being able to climb out of the compartment and, once again, go turn on the bilge pump.

After several hours, I was ready to repack the shaft by taking apart the stuffing gland and pounding in two more pieces of Teflon packing. I tightened down the stuffing gland and watched the stream being reduced to a dribble and then drops, and finally, there was no leakage at all.

I cleaned up my tools and hoisted the staysail, and we were off again, moving nicely towards our turn that was down around 35° south latitude and a longitude of 135° west. There, we would actually get headed for Cape Horn and start our east-around passage. This entire chain of events had taken eight hours to get things back in order. I was extremely exhausted and feeling all alone thousands of miles from any-anywhere. Suddenly, a feeling came over me that I was not alone, and I felt a presence onboard. The hair began to stand up on the back of my neck as I moved about Sailors Run, checking every conceivable spot one could hide. This presence was so thick and heavy I felt I could reach out and touch it. After what had to have been forty minutes, it all went away, and once again, I knew I was alone, far out to sea. Who or what it was I do not know, but I can assure you I had company for about forty minutes.

DAY 16

I awoke to a loud screeching noise outside in the cockpit. I climbed out into the cockpit, looking around for what was getting ready to go bad next. Then I heard the noise coming from aloft off the stern of the boat. There, I was amazed to see five white Birds of Paradise soaring and kicking up the biggest fuss. I thought possibly they were warning of some impending danger, but nothing was found, and I could only wonder where they came from and where they were going. Perhaps they were wondering the same thing!

Today, I started fishing by dragging a pink squid on a meat line, a heavy 200-pound test line on a rubber snubber. Since I found so many pink squid on the boat, I figured, "Why not try one?"

After the squalls seemed to let up, it was time to shake out the reef in the mainsail. I went to release the reef line at the mast and was shocked to see it had chafed through 95% of the way. The line was brand new, and the reef had been tied in for only about 12 days. I ended up having to use the fish tape to pull in a new 45-foot piece of ½ inch line. I also made some changes in the bottom of the boom configuration that I believe will eliminate the chafe.

DAY 17

I want to thank everyone for their great ideas on solving the shaft problem; they are noteworthy. I'm glad to have the technology that makes it possible to receive them via email on the single-sideband radio. Also, thanks for the prayers and encouragement.

One idea was to put thread-lock on the threads. I should have thought of this one, as I have plenty of it. I fear my thought processes were on overload as I worked with a stream of water pouring into the bilge. Another great idea was to put epoxy on the shaft and hand-tighten the nut. That would definitely fix it. A more aggressive idea was to fill the coupler with epoxy and pray you die before you ever have to take out the shaft! A truly quick temporary fix is to put a shaft Zinc inside the boat right up against the packing gland. This one I tried but only had collar zincs, and the diameter was too wide, so the zinc hit the packing gland bolts. If I had the torpedo zinc, it would have worked.

What I did do was split a piece of heavy duty hose that was the same inside diameter as the shaft and then hose clamp it onto the shaft tight up against the packing gland. This held things in place until I eventually got the nut secured with thread-lock. If the nut was to come off again, this should keep the shaft from sliding out of the coupler for a little while.

Today, I'm dragging a cedar plug lure for the fish, as I had no luck with the squid.

DAY 18

Current Stats
Position
Lat. 28°24'S / Long. 111°46'W
Weather
Barometer = 1018 mb. -- Wind = 8-15 kts. -- Temp = 71°-75°
Seas
5-7 ft.
Distance
24 hr. run = 157 NM
Miles sailed last three days = 463 NM
Total miles sailed so far = 2672 NM
Miles left to go to turning point for the Horn = 585 NM
Top speed so far
9.9 kts.

This morning, Easter Island lays 48 NM off the port beam. I am sad I didn't get close enough to see it, but the wind gods are dictating I sail more to the west to get over the top of the high.

Yes, it's almost barometer soup time. As you might have noticed, the barometric pressure is gradually rising as I near the center of the South Pacific high. I do not want to cross the center, as there will be no wind or little fluky winds. The problem is the high wanders around, and yesterday, it was centered on longitude 111°. Today it is at 113°, and I want it to go back to 111° or even further east. I can only hope the 120° longitude is far enough west for me to be able to skirt along the outside edge of the high to a point where I pick up the westerly winds that are currently at about 40° south.

Still trying to catch a fish—the Jefe'.

DAY 19

After 18 days, the lithium batteries in my Spot locator are dead, and I had to replace them with alkaline batteries. We will now find out how well they hold up. Today, I also put a cedar plug in the water, hoping to pick up a fish to fill the empty freezer space.

Have you ever gone on vacation when suddenly you are overcome with this dreadful feeling that you have forgotten something very important? Today, I realized I have forgotten to purchase two hot water bottles that I had expected to help get me through the cold of the Southern Ocean, as I have no provisions for heating the boat. At first, this seemed like a huge loss, as a hot water bottle will keep you warm for about five hours in your berth. Of course, necessity is the mother of invention, and after sleeping on this problem for a night, I came up with a solution. I took an empty 1.75-liter tequila bottle, found a fuzzy fender cover to wrap around that bottle, filled it with hot water, and used a cork for a plug. Suddenly, I was back in business as far as a bed warmer goes.

DAY 20

Today, I ate my last orange and will be switching to apples for my daily fruit. I'm not the greatest cook in the galley, as Debbie, my wife, is an excellent cook, and I pale in her presence, but out here, I have to do my best, and fortunately for me, I'm not hard to please. I keep it simple, just cooking two meals a day. Breakfast might be cold cereal, fruit, and of course coffee. Dinner always involves cooking, and a piece of meat is generally fried, with a salad, and for desert, it is usually cookies and tea or perhaps a piece of dark chocolate. Also, a rum drink while cooking makes it much more enjoyable. I have about two more weeks of meat left onboard.

Back on deck, I have to duck behind the dodger, as frequent cold showers of water are permeating the air as we are blasting along close to the wind, sailing our course line. My favorite time of the day is at the conclusion of the 24-hour run, when I get to add up our miles traveled and plot it on the paper charts. At least then I can see some progress towards realizing my dream.

DAY 21

Winds are down, and this morning, I pulled myself up the mizzenmast to tear apart the wind generator as we were making less than five knots on fairly smooth seas. I pulled off the blades, a real juggling act on a rolling boat in a boson's chair. Then I removed the nut from the generator shaft and soon had it in one hand and the three-blade prop in the other. Now, I find myself trying to figure out what the f**k to do, as I sway back in forth in the bosun's chair, safely strapped to the mast. Next, I pull the three screws out of the faceplate, pull that off and let it dangle with half the generator in it from the three wires that go to the brains of the thing. I cleaned the slip rings with a Scotch pad and noticed a bare wire that could have been the culprit causing it not to work all the time. A little electrical tape cured that. I sweat bullets until the whole thing is all screwed and bolted back together again. Of course, there is not enough air to turn it now, so I don't know if it is fixed yet, but I know for sure I'm done working on it! Pretty soon, the wind picks up, and the wind generator still does not work. I'm sorry to think it, but I'm afraid it is out of the picture for the rest of the voyage.

I have a lot of time to think and reminisce out here on the ocean. I was thinking about what an old sailing friend of mine once told me about extending your fuel range with a diesel motor. He had worked at a refining company and swore you could dilute the diesel with 15% gasoline if you had it and extend your range and not damage your engine. So, being the thinker I am, I wondered if, when one of my rum bottles gets down to about 15%, I could use some of that big bottle of rubbing alcohol I have in the medicine cabinet to extend my range a bit! Then I was thinking, if my water maker quits working, while I still have water, should every fourth glass of water that I drink be salt water, thereby extending my range, or maybe it would just be best to drink the gasoline!

I found out the Kirkland alkaline batteries only lasted three days in the spot locator before needing to be replaced, so I will only be turning it on about every eight hours to send out my position.

Sorting it all out in the Pacific, your Amigo, the Jefe'.

DAY 22

This morning, when I went topside, I discovered that one of the steering lines to the wind vane was chafing. This was an easy fix once I switched the steering over to the electronic autopilot—now, I could get slack in the line on the wind vane and tie a new figure eight knot at the servo rudder getting beyond the chafed area.

Today, I tried to estimate my arrival times off each of the five great capes and eventual arrival back at the start. I knew this was a very complex equation with way too many variables to be truly accurate. My guess was Cape Horn on December 12th and I decided to quit at that. Who knows what might happen between here and there? All I know is that 150 total days is my dream.

DAY 23

Today, we are sailing very slowly, and it is the day that I had hoped to reach our turning point for the Horn. The only problem is, if I tack over now, we will be headed into the center of the high where little wind could be found, so we remain on the port tack going to the SW, away from the Horn.

Last night, while rolling up the fishing line on the notched piece of wood I use, I was shocked as I got a strike on the lure, and my hand was yanked back hard into the stern pulpit.

Wow, I always wondered what that would feel like, and I'm here to tell you it hurts like hell.

DAY 24

Today the wind is down, making lounging in the cockpit very comfortable. Traveling at a very slow rate of speed makes fishing unlikely to be a success, so I'm shocked when we suddenly hook a beautiful, big eye tuna. I slowly work him up alongside the boat on the meat line, where finally I can slam the gaff home and haul him aboard. Blood is flying everywhere as I struggle to get him back behind the wheel, where I can release him and feel pretty confident the fish won't bounce over the side of the boat. The fish weighed in at 15 pounds, and after it was filleted, I had 14 more dinners and a full freezer—once again, "Yahoo!"

I must admit the fix on the shaft coupling has been bothering me. There was no way to get that nut on the end of the shaft tight enough to feel good about the hold. With the slow sailing, I decide to separate the coupling, once again, and slide the shaft back. While freewheeling along under sail, I mix up a handful of Marine-Tex and pack the coupling full of it, so the nut cannot possibly spin off the shaft again. I believe the bolts that hold the coupling together could fall out and the coupling would stay together, bonded by the Marine-Tex.

DAY 25

Barometer is on the way down, and that is good, as the high is moving out, and the wind will be filling in. As I watched over the stern, gazing down into the clear blue ocean, I see several fish following the boat. One appeared about two feet long and had black and gray stripes running around his body. The other fish was brown and looked like a 10" trout. I also noticed some Blue Bottle jellyfish. They are unusual, as they stay on the surface and have a sail they hoist when wanting to move around. They are about 5" long, and the sail sticks up about 3-4". I pulled out one with a net once and was surprised to see a single very long tentacle hanging down that I was told hurts like hell if you are stung by it.

DAY 26

I have been creeping along the 120° longitude for 3 days, and it is refreshing to see the winds start to fill back in. I'm sure, if I had any hair, I would have surely pulled it all out by now!

I have a solar panel issue that I'm mulling over. The panels are doing a great job keeping the batteries charged up, but two of them are hanging out on my one-inch stainless steel rails. They are 2 x 4 feet, presenting a large area not only to the sun but the seas as well. I planned to pull them off when the seas got up, but now that the wind generator is out, I'm thinking about maybe leaving one on and putting the other below. The panels are fused, so if they were destroyed, the fuse should blow.

On my last trip down this way in 2008, there were many sunny days even when a gale was blowing. This is an El Nino year, so not sure what to expect. The only difference so far is that the South Pacific High has moved south sooner this year, or so it seems to me.

DAY 27

Current Stats
Position
Lat. 40°16'S / Long. 118°38'W
Weather
Barometer = 1006 mb. -- Wind = 8-25 kts. - - Temp = 71°-77°
Seas
8-10 ft.

Distance
24 hr. run = 117 NM
Miles sailed last three days = 289 NM
Total miles sailed so far = 3640 NM
Distance left to go to the Horn = 2210 NM

Top speed so far
9.9 kts.

I want to wish all of you a belated Happy Thanksgiving, "...if you know what I mean, Pilgrims." My dinner was chicken fried in a sesame batter with boiled potatoes and a can of green beans. That will be the first can I have opened on this voyage, if you don't count the Budweiser I had for dessert.

Today, we are nicely corkscrewing our way along, with the wind coming from astern and freshening. I reefed the staysail and hoisted it back up, giving me options in heavy weather where I can roll the genoa almost all the way in and still be powered up nicely.

We had a big squall come through about 3 am, blowing about 35 knots. I had to put two reefs in the main, and the mizzen is down, covered on the boom. It makes it tough to sail fast all the time when the wind velocity changes so drastically, like I'm experiencing.

Here, we are doing the "Turkey Trot" along the way to the Horn.

DAY 28

Welcome to the roaring 40's, and yes, they are roaring at times. Right now, I'm just trying to get the boat dialed in. The hardest part is that the squalls are packing 35 knots, and I'm normally trying to sail in 10-15 knots. I pulled down the mizzen, as it tends to make the boat corkscrew around too much when the squalls come in over our stern. I reefed the staysail, giving me lots of options up front, and last night at 3 am, in an exceptionally bad squall, I double-reefed the main. We are definitely starting to have fun now. We half-filled the cockpit twice today when steep waves broke in over Sailors Run's stern.

DAY 29

Today was the hardest day of the trip, as there is a 964 mb low that has formed several hundred miles NE of me. I'm getting hammered with SE winds and severe seas, making going towards my destination nearly impossible. After sailing 125 nautical miles, we only made good about 25 toward our destination, the Horn. Along the way, the rope drum on the steering wheel was falling off as two of the three hose clamps that hold it on had broken. There is no way to replace those clamps when the wheel is spinning back and forth, so I put the boat on electric autopilot and took off the wheel. That became rather painful, as the last time I tried to pull off the wheel in Argentina, it would not come off. Anticipating the problem, I took off the nut, sat down behind the wheel, and gave it the most powerful yank I could come up with. I could not believe how easily it flew off the shaft and smacked this "Yank" right in the head. Holy shit! I saw stars for a minute, but luckily, I have a hard head. Once I got the wheel below, it was easy to replace the broken hose clamps. Later in the afternoon, I altered course to SW, as it looks like the low is dropping down on me. I'm going to get out of its way and jump on the backside of it as it comes down, allowing us to have favorable winds to head for the Horn.

DAY 30

Today was yet another "worst day of the trip." The low has moved right down on top of me, and I am seeing 30 to 50 knots and "rough ass" seas. They are not so big that I fear being rolled, but they have done some damage. We are currently hove-to with broken steering cables. I still have cabbage, onions, potatoes, squash, apples, and oh yeah, an extra couple pieces of steering cable! The steering wheel spins much like the "Wheel of Fortune"! I have just won another non-paid repair in confined spaces! Oh, and by the way, the steering cables were replaced just 8 months ago, and I have never, ever broken one in 22 years—and change them regularly every 5 years.

I cannot use the wind vane until repairs are made to the steering cables, so that puts it pretty high on the priority list. I can steer with the electronic autopilot for now. Once this low moves off and we are sailing towards our destination, not taking seas aboard in the cockpit, I will make the repair. Things are getting wet below, as the waves that are breaking on the boat are breaching the seal on the overhead butterfly hatch. If it gets much wetter below, I will have to wear my rain gear to sit at the table on the not-so-dry cushions. After one month, I am already starting to grow gills!

Sailors Run under sail headed for the starting line off of Bahia
Caraquez, Ecuador.

Sailors Run heading out for solo circumnavigation.

Big Eye Tuna just in time to fill up freezer, once again.

Sailors Run on a beam reach to get out of harm's way.

Sailors Run caught in first big storm 30 days out.

Chapter 6: Days 31-60

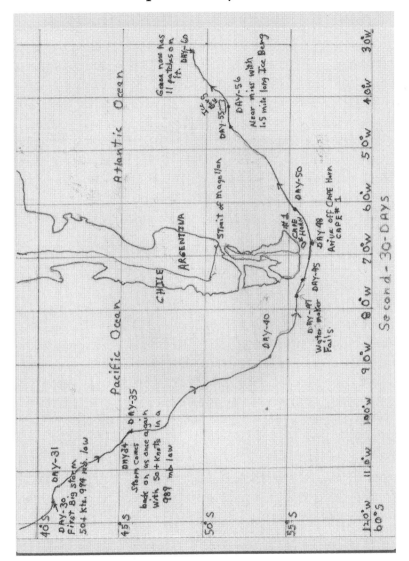

DAY 31

The 964 mb low is still nearly on top of us. The worst of it came at about 1 in the morning when the winds were screeching at 50 knots and lasted until three a.m. The only good thing to come out of it was the winds seemed to flatten the seas somewhat, so there were smaller holes to crash down into! The sailing conditions are severe enough that alarm bells are going off in my head as we battle large turbulent seas with one major problem; the steering cables failed and can't be dealt with until conditions moderate somewhat. The waves are still breaking into the cockpit at times, so repairs will not be attempted on steering cables. So just know, I'm missing those nice warm winters along the "Gold Coast" of Mexico.

At last, we are starting to sail over the top of the low as it is moving SW, and now, I can at least steer the course to the Horn.

DAY 32

The winds are down, and it is time to see if the steering cables can be fixed. I estimate, if things go well, it should take about three hours, Hmmmmmm! The chain had spun off the sprocket, dropping down inside the steering pedestal. I removed the compass, disconnected the fuel and shift cable, so I could pry up that part of the pedestal and get under it with my fish tape. I hoped to be able to hook the chain or a cable and drag it out. After about twenty minutes, I was still unsuccessful at dragging out the chain. Even after it was hooked, it was impossible because you have to get it around the sprocket, the steering shaft, and then the brake mechanism for the wheel. I stepped back and decided that, possibly, I could unbolt everything on top of the wheel tube and lift that off, then I would have a four-inch opening out of which to drag the chain and cables.

Now you must picture, we are sailing in some large waves, and two of my biggest compartments had to be emptied into the cockpit. This means there are 1000 feet of lines, different lengths of chain, a 60 lb. CQR anchor, 5 gallons of oil, transmission oil, hoses, electrical cords, Hookah hose, and many other miscellaneous things. I don't know, "why the hell I have all this shit." OK, so you get the picture. All work is done with the hatches open and piles of shit everywhere. That means you must walk on it, lay on it, and most importantly, try to keep it from falling down into the open hatches to the bilge where things can disappear forever.

Once I get all the bolts out of the steering shaft housing, there seems to be no way to get it off the four-inch stainless steel tube. It is bronze, and you can only pound on that stuff so much. Three hours—what was I thinking? Well, if you can't get it from the top, why not the bottom? I crawled down in the compartment and took off the four nuts that hold the bronze cable wheels and the backing plate for the steering pedestal. Suddenly, I have the chain and cables in my hand! As a matter of fact, the cable broke right at the chain, and there was enough extra wire at the steering quadrant end to remake it onto the chain using two Crosby U-bolt clamps.

In the end, it took seven hours with no breaks. Steady work, but I can tell you I feel much better today knowing it is fixed. I believe it failed because the lines to the wind vane steering became too slack and allowed the rudder to swing back and forth. The wind vane would stop the wheel from spinning suddenly, allowing the chain to cut into the cable. Or, possibly, it was the result of the shaft sliding out of the coupling and back against the rudder, requiring a lot of extra pressure to turn the rudder.

DAY 33

A nice sailing day, and I finally got up enough nerve to take the transmission out of reverse and let the prop spin while I ran the boat in neutral, circulating the oil and basically drying out the engine for twenty minutes. Next, I started the water maker and ran it for an hour, making water. The water maker produces about 7 gallons an hour. I consume, on average, about 2.5 gallons a day. Our first 75-gallon tank ran dry after thirty days, so I will gradually top off both tanks. It certainly feels good sailing, once again, with a boat you can steer!

DAY 34

I awoke this morning to the sound of water rushing alongside the hull. The boat was gyrating as it was skipping up and over the waves, which had grown overnight. A quick glance at the barometer showed a substantial drop in pressure. It appears the low that passed over us two days ago was coming back for a second go, but this time, it should be with a more favorable wind direction, helping drive us to the Horn. "Hang On!"

It seems very cool this morning as I put the coffee on the stove for a much-needed warm up. "What the Hell?!" The damn thing won't light. I go out into the all-too-brisk 25 knots and hoist the tank. "Huh!" it has gas in it. Back down below, I pull the fuse on the solenoid switch, and it appears fine. Oh well, it's early; perhaps I should try lighting it again. I try to no avail, except I smell gas, so I shut off the solenoid valve at the tank. I rock the stove forward on its gimbals and inspect the gas line coming into the stove—oh my God! The copper line that connects to the flexible hose has broken off! So, when I turned on the gas, it was flowing into the galley, not into the burner on the stove. I was just trying to light the wrong area. If I would have lowered the lighter, I surely would have been able to get things warmed up. Now, if that wasn't a near "Catastrophic Blast," I don't know what is!

After going out on deck twice and reefing the main, then having to take it all the way down, once again, I was back below to get the stove operating. I use my Makita cutting blade, cut off the bent, and smashed portions of the copper supply line, then slip a piece of rubber gas line over the two ends of copper pipe. Using sealant and hose clamps, the copper pipes were soon rejoined, and now, I have a working stove once again. A jury-rig for sure but hopefully safe enough to get us home. I finally have coffee at 11 a.m. and breakfast by noon; plus, I have put in a day's work.

DAY 35

Today, the waves have come down a little, and the ride has improved. The barometer has also fallen. It is interesting as I plot our course and progress on my old paper chart. I see we are on the same track for the run into the Horn, as the Vendee Globe Boats were in their solo around-the-world race back in 2008-09. We are right behind where Fonica was on 1/1/09 and just ahead of the boat Roxy's position.

Last night, I threw the heavy llama-hair blanket on my berth, as it feels like it is freezing at night, of course, not really, but it feels that way. Debbie bought that blanket in Peru; it weighs about 20 lbs. and is truly a life saver, especially when you throw that 1.75-liter tequila bottle full of hot water in there with you to get things warmed up.

The Jefe'

Current Stats

Position
Lat. 48°00'S / Long. 100°48'W

Weather
Barometer = 989 mb. -- Wind = 18-30 kts. - - Temp = 51°-60°

Seas
8-13 ft.

Distance
24 hr. run = 154 NM
Miles sailed last three days = 454 NM
Total miles sailed so far = 4817 NM
Distance left to go to the Horn = 1952 NM

Top speed so far
10.9 kts.

Today finds us pretty much on course for the run into the Horn. With over 1400 NM to go, it will be a long, wild "roller coaster" ride. I hope and pray, because I'm nearly a month ahead of when I rounded the Horn last time in 2009, to make it before the first big summer storm. Down here, they have the worst storms in the summer, and I need to steer clear of those no matter what ocean I'm in.

The off-shore approach to the Horn from the west is a big, long commitment, with 8 to 10 days spent below 46°S, and each day moving further to the south, the air and water temperatures drop. Then add 90% humidity and a chill factor created by 300 gales a year at the Horn and you will be trying to figure out some way to keep from freezing off that big set of balls that it takes to come this way in the first place. I have two beer cozies and am sewing them together. Maybe this will work out for me!

DAY 37

I took down the mizzen overnight, and this morning, I'm sailing with a double-reefed main and a third of the genoa. It is gusting over 25 knots, I'm cold, and down here anything warm to eat or drink helps raise my core temperature.

Resting and sleeping are very difficult down here. As you lie in your bunk, you hear about fifteen different noises: cans shifting in the bilge, water rushing by the hull, the block that pops on deck if the genoa gets a little slack, the fire extinguisher that lets you know it's there by banging on the cabinet where it is hanging, it goes on and on. Once you decide there is no new noise that might mean springing into action, you tune out all the above and concentrate on your equilibrium and pressure placed on different parts of your body. Finally, you calm down and can fall asleep, but if the pressure anywhere on your body changes or your equilibrium picks up on a different motion, you will wake up. I have come to realize the tequila bottle is also a good clock, as when it gets lukewarm, it is time to get up. The safest, warmest, and my most favorite place on the boat is in my berth behind the lee-cloth.

DAY 38

That low pressure coming back to take another shot at Sailors Run seems to be staying to the south and moving through below us. We should only see 25 to 30 knots, but there is a severe weather warning associated with it for 40 knots, gusting 50 to 60 knots and severe seas, which I hope not to experience. The Horn looks to be about one week out, and if we are lucky, we will arrive right behind a big low. The problem is, we must get so far south that we will have to weather any low that comes, but better *before* the Horn than at the Horn.

The gap between the tip of South America and Antarctica is just over 300 miles wide, creating a narrow area where these lows tend to pass through, and there is a shelf that extends out sixty miles off the tip of South America that must be avoided in severe weather.

Today, I did two small loads of laundry, getting most of the water blown out of it before bringing it inside to finish drying. It takes days to dry at 51°F.

DAY 39

Sailors Run was being driven hard before the wind with the mizzen back up, so during increasing winds this morning, I dropped the mizzen. It was then I noticed one of the small nylon socket pieces had disappeared, and at the gooseneck, the boom had come out of its socket. Now I must manufacture another one or improvise. I have an idea about using some hose material to pick up the slop between the bottom and the top of the boom jaws. I have a French rig, and it is very different from most mizzen goosenecks. I rebuilt the main gooseneck less than a year ago, and it appears now I should have done this one as well.

I also noticed the 7 to 8-inch piece of 3-inch diameter fire hose that I had clamped on the main engine exhaust has been washed away by a large wave. I had it there to discourage large waves from forcing water into the exhaust system. To replace it means hanging by my toes over the stern of the boat and working in icy cold water. "Brrr!"

I don't remember mentioning that, during 50 knots in the low, about a week ago, my Windex wind direction indicator blew off the top of the mast, so now it is much harder to see the wind at night. I used to get a visual on that from inside the boat with the tri-color illuminating it. Now, we are back to tell-tales on the stainless-steel rigging. I heard the coldest winter you will ever spend is a summer in San Francisco, but now I believe that to be wrong; it has to be a summer in the Southern Ocean!

The Jefe', "Hauling Ass" for the Horn.

DAY 40

The weather looks good for the next three days, but down here, I don't trust it! I tried fishing, but the birds were all over my lure, so I pulled it in rather than risk catching one. The Albatross and Terns are fun to watch as they glide over the large waves with little effort. I was putting the cover on the mizzen and a sea tern flew up and hovered about three feet from my face and watched me as he exhibited no fear. The other thing about catching a fish is trying to fillet it, as both you and the fish slide around the cockpit with a very sharp knife in your hand. The tuna in the can is looking better all the time!

DAY 41

I'm fishing again this morning while the barometer plummets, and it is very cold at 42°. When I was here 6 years ago, the coldest temperature I recorded was 45 degrees. I also had hail in the cockpit in the morning, and it was snowing an icy snow when I was on deck making sail changes. Now, with "global warming" and it being an El Nino year, it's pretty hard to figure out what is going on! Another interesting phenomenon is the cooking oil I bought in Ecuador has jelled out, and you must shake it out of the bottle like ketchup. Possibly, I just need to add 15% antifreeze to remedy this situation, and that would no doubt help reduce any potential cholesterol buildup.

One of my greatest fears is becoming injured or ill while far out to sea. I must admit, the heavy clothing I must wear adds protection for those short flights across the cabin by rogue waves. Today, I took a knife and went to free a beer from a plastic wrapped 6-pack in the beer locker, when suddenly, Sailors Run dropped off a wave, causing me to slash a 5-inch gash in the side of a beer. That is one beer I will never get to drink, and I got a shower at the same time. Now, the boat smells like one of those pubs I used to frequent!

A gale blew up about 4 p.m., and the seas began to build. The wind vane was steering, and I was below, when suddenly, the boat turned up into the wind, and we ended up lying abeam to some very large waves. I dashed into the cockpit, just wearing my jacket, and noticed the steering line to the wind-vane had come off the drum at the wheel. I disengaged the wind vane and spun the wheel to steer downwind, putting these monster waves on our stern. Then I locked in the electric autopilot to steer a safer course, while I figured out how to remedy the situation of the line coming off the drum.

The gale was continuing to worsen. There were many powerful squalls within it pushing the winds near 50 knots at times, and some of the waves appeared to be a good 30 feet high. I decided to stay on the electric autopilot overnight, hoping to get some sleep. The night went pretty well, but at 6 a.m., we were hit by a large rogue wave coming in on our beam. I just sat down in my berth with a cup of coffee and had one foot up on the seating around the table and one on the table. The next thing I know, I'm standing straight up, and things are flying everywhere. I could see the port side windows down by my feet awash, and then Sailors Run righted herself just as quickly as she had been knocked down. I figure we went over no more than 90°, and I doubt the mast went in the water, but it was a pretty unnerving and unexpected knock down. I had a huge mess to clean up, and one drawer that had flown out had cracked the wood on the face of it. Some water had also found its way below through the main hatch, but it was only a small amount. The current outlook is for the weather to calm down over the next 24 hours, and I surely hope so.

DAY 42

I remedied the drum problem at the wheel by using smaller line at that location, and it seems to be working much more reliably. I hoisted the reefed staysail and rolled the genoa all the way in until weather conditions improve. I got the hose back on the exhaust to keep out waves and made a temporary fix on the mizzen gooseneck.

It is still snowing a sort of sleet in the squalls, and I will be glad to reach the Horn and be able to get a little north and out of this coldest of cold conditions. It will be nice to get the Horn out of the way early in our circumnavigation.

Hanging in there, the Jefe'.

DAY 43

The day started nice, so it was time to try fishing once again. It has become obvious that the water maker is having trouble starting, and I suspect a bad electrical connection. It is also time to water the wet cell batteries, as I do this every two months. I emptied all the "stuff" out of the outside compartment to gain access to the water maker and, of course, had to empty out the quarter-berth to gain access to the batteries. Now, it is simple to run two new wires from the water maker directly to the batteries. I touched the new wires directly to the batteries, expecting to hear the water maker come to life. WRONG, the large electric motor will not go. It's amazing how these things unfold, as today is a great sailing day, but I must reduce sail, so I can pull out the water maker and tear into the electric motor.

I lay out rags all over the galley floor, and there with me, the water maker, and my tools all slide around together as I tear into it. This electric motor is a wet one, meaning it has heavy oil inside it, a MESS! The armature shows lots of wear from the past 14 years of making water, so I clean it up the best I can with a scotch pad, and the brushes still appear to be OK. Seven hours later, the water maker is reinstalled, and it's time for the smoke test. Yes, you guessed it, the "F**K**G" thing does not work. So I'm inquiring about "dry martini" recipes and a way to cook rice without water. Possibly, it is time to add 15% salt water to my remaining 80 gallons of fresh water to extend its life. I can't help but wonder just how much fresh water I might be able to salvage out of those two big squash I have if I just beat the shit out of them with a baseball bat! OK,

The Jefe'

OK, I will catch water on deck, and I have a hand-operated water maker in my ditch bag, but it is very small and very labor intensive.

DAY 44

Wind has gone light, 7 to 12 knots, but there are still occasional squalls, so the spinnaker remains below for now! It is frustrating being so close to the Horn and just creeping along.

Debbie is doing great in Albuquerque, decorating the house inside and out with Christmas lights and many other decorations. She says she actually got a blanket of snow the other night, so that's pretty cool, and she is excited about cheering on her Seattle Sea Hawks football team.

DAY 45

Current Stats
Position
Lat. 56°17'S / Long. 7°33'W
Weather
Barometer = 996 mb. -- Wind = 0-12 kts. - - Temp = 44°-51°
Seas
2-4 ft.

Distance
24 hr. run = 71 NM
Miles sailed last three days = 303 NM
Total miles sailed so far = 5997 NM
Miles left to go to the Horn = 247 NM

Top speed so far
12.2 kts.

This morning, the spinnaker went up, as the weather looks very benign, and it was the first day I nearly spent all day out in the cockpit. We sailed for 10 hours under spinnaker, then at 6 p.m., the wind just died, and the ocean glassed off. It was 2:30 a.m. before the wind came back, and now it is pretty much on the nose, so currently, we are pounding to weather trying to get to the Horn.

Singing "How dry I am. How dry I am. Nobody knows how dry I am."

DAY 46

Still beating to weather to get to the Horn, and on the good tack, I can only steer within 30 degrees of the course line. Today is a milestone for me, as in 2009, after 45 days, I arrived in Buenos Aires, Argentina after sailing from Lima, Peru around the Horn solo. I arrived at one in the morning, and it was blowing a gale. I had broken my hand, and I was to sail into the Marina through a very narrow gated entrance. All in all, I was pretty much a basket case for many reasons, but I have to admit, today on this voyage, a much larger one by about 5 times, after 45 days, I feel good. Once I get past the Horn, it will be a relief, as I can move a little further north where the temperature should warm up about 5 degrees.

DAY 47

Land Ho! I can see the snow-capped mountains of Chile. I have been forced north of the Horn. Now, I must tack along the coast of Chile to get to the Horn, which means less sleep and a much more intense watch system. A low is coming in to the south of me, and by Day 49, we should have 30 knots of favorable breeze to sail past the Horn. The weather has been out of the norm, with much calmer conditions than normal.

I had a problem with the way the wind vane was steering and determined the gears were meshing too loosely, causing it to be less responsive. Working on a wind vane at sea is not a good idea, especially if you have to pull out a shaft because there are lots of little roller bearings that can disappear on you. So, to get the slop out of the gear on top of the servo rudder, I cut a very large 2.5-inch washer in half with my Makita cutting wheel and then slipped both halves of the stainless-steel washer under the gear, getting rid of the slop. Then I took a hose clamp and secured the two halves in place, and it works perfectly—fixed!

DAY 48

This morning, while tacking along the coast of Chile, a very large blue whale surfaced and blew alongside Sailors Run. A whale nearly 100 feet long tends to make me and my boat feel very small.

Some people have asked what I eat out here. Well, it goes like this: Breakfast is one egg, fried potatoes and onions plus coffee, or coffee and one bowl of Special-K cereal with granola, or coffee with oatmeal and raisins. Lunch is just a snack and one adult beverage. The snack is usually a small package of crackers and a couple of slices of cheese. Dinner is early, about 4 P.M., and has been stir-fried cabbage and onions with either a hamburger patty, a chicken breast, or a filet of fish. This is all cooked in one small frying pan. Now my diet is about to change, as I only have 4 dinners left in the freezer. Soon, it will be canned tuna, canned veggies, soups and stews, unless I catch another fish. I still have about 15 apples, some onions, and potatoes, along with the two large squash that are stashed next to the baseball bat. I also have a cup of tea about 7 p.m. with a small package of cookies while I read a book. I don't think I have gained or lost weight so far, but I expect I shall before it is all over. I'm just eating my way around the world.

Later in the afternoon, I had a pod of very large dolphins with white bellies doing amazing jumps and flips out of the water just off my bow. Sometime later, I noticed a fish jumping but under closer observation, it turned out to be a penguin. He hung around the boat for about an hour. I tried feeding him crackers, but he was not at all impressed.

DAY 49

"CAPE HORN AT LAST"

After 49 days and 2 hours, Sailors Run arrives off the most rugged and beautiful cape in the world. Through the tear-blurred eyes, I can barely see it, even though it is less than 5 miles away. I shudder when I think I have, once again, been granted safe passage to this amazing place. It seems as though nature has caused me to linger along the Chilean coast as I beat my way to the Horn in light winds. Being slowed by nature and forced north, I saw some of the most amazing sea life that presented itself to me as I "worried" my way down to the Horn. Now I'm here at last. I want to thank my wife Debbie for all her wonderful support and to all our family and great friends for their prayers and emotional support in this huge undertaking. I also must thank Robert Perry for designing such an outstanding cruising boat, the Baba 40 ketch, and those of you that have donated gear and money to help make all of this possible, and to all my Amigos, much thanks.

Now, we rapidly sail clear of the Horn into the depths of the Atlantic and all it has in store for us. The next leg will be about 3000 nautical miles to a point nearly 1000 miles south of the "Cape of Good Hope" at Latitude 48° south.

DAY 50

After a day of rocketing away from the Horn, in winds up to 30 knots that were created by a low that slipped below us to the south, it is once again time to pay my dues. On the eve of a heavy weather sailing day, during an inspection of the genoa sail, I noticed three new tears in the sail. I furled in the sail to cover the torn area. Down here, it starts getting light at 1:00 a.m. Bahía Caraquez time, and at 2:30 a.m., I rolled out the genoa sail and glued patches over the tears. I could just barely reach the tears while standing on the bow pulpit, lashed onto the furled part of the sail with my safety harness. Once again, I furled the sail, allowing the contact cement to set. At 6 a.m., I pulled the genoa down off the furler tube and spread it out on deck, where I could complete a proper repair. I glued on additional patches that backed up the first patches that were already installed on the opposite side of the sail then sewed the patches together, all the time sliding about on the fore deck, harnessed into my jack line. I'm very thankful for a high toe rail to brace myself against and stop me from sliding off the deck. After about one and a half hours, the sail was back up and flying at 100% as we waited for the winds to build.

Sailing on a passage such as this is like having a new baby in your home. There is no set routine, and you never know when nature [baby] will call. I should mention that, as of this day, I believe we are nearly 30% complete on our solo circumnavigation. Yahoo!

DAY 51

The sun is out, and the winds have returned, making this day tolerable to be outside. It seems, when the wind comes from the north, the temperature is nearly 10 degrees warmer than the southerly winds off Antarctica. I take advantage of the good conditions to put out a fishing line and do a much-needed outside project. I moved the double cheek block, through which the control lines from the wind-vane pass, aft about half an inch. I believe this change will stop the steering line from dropping off the wheel again.

A cedar plug was my choice for the fishing lure, as it runs a little deeper, so the Albatross can't get it, as they do not dive below the surface. You can imagine my surprise when I came on deck to see five giant albatrosses trying to get my lure. My first instinct was to grab the camera, but then I saw what these guys were up to. They would fly right up near the stern of Sailors Run where the line entered the water and grab the fishing line in one of their beaks. The one with the line in his beak slipped aft towards the lure as it was leveraged up to the surface, and all the birds could get after it. I grabbed the meat line and started pulling it in, all the time trying to scare away the birds to no avail. Suddenly, the lure got to the albatross and somehow hooked him or tangled him in the line. I knew the bird would surely drown if I did not haul him in and try to set him free. I know from experience you do not want to attempt this without first putting on gloves because those suckers bite hard. The bird was towing in pretty well, when suddenly, it turned over, creating a huge drag on the line. I was shocked at what happened next. The bird reached out with his beak, bit the leader in half, and suddenly took flight. Now whether he caught or swallowed the lure was not evident as he flew very well and circled the area looking perfectly normal. That was the end of the cedar plug and my attempt to fish on this day.

From deep in the Atlantic, your amigo the Jefe'.

DAY 52

Today was an amazing day, as I had no projects to do, so in the morning, I cleaned up the boat and decided to take a shower. The showers are only being done every fourth day now to conserve water, and I'm still trying to figure out how to take one with my long-underwear on, being it's so cold, but still no luck on that.

I felt great after the shower, washed all the dishes and put them away, and it seemed like a good time to sit down with my Kindle and read a mystery story. After what must have been twenty minutes, I noticed the boat's motion had changed, and it seemed that the wind vane might not be steering. Once out in the cockpit, I was shocked to see what looked like a large silver salmon swimming just behind the boat. Upon closer examination, this was no salmon at all but the shiny servo rudder off the Monitor wind vane, trailing behind on its safety line. Now this was all as it should be, as the thinner coupler tube connecting the rudder to the wind vane had broken off, as it should when something rolls up from under the boat, like a log etc. I just hoped it wasn't my rudder leaving that had done it, as I had not heard us hit a log.

I dug through my compartments, and on the third one, I came up with a couple of replacement pieces of stainless steel tubing to make the repair. Once again, with the Makita cutting wheel leading the charge, and the Milwaukee drill punching out the holes, soon a replacement had appeared right before my eyes. Bolting it back on was the interesting part, as we were sailing fast, and the stern wake was up around the bolt that had to be removed and then replaced after the new tube was inserted in the hinge socket. Once again, I found myself tethered off, hanging by my knees off the back of the boat, working in frigid waters to make the installation happen. Fixed, it appeared the breaking of the wind vane was metal fatigue, more than any one big hit.

DAY 53

Today, the Sailors Run is challenged by light and variable winds from many different directions, and this always makes for lots of work trying to keep the boat moving in the right direction. It appears we are in the middle of a low and must wait for it to move over us, hopefully taking off on the backside of it.

I installed a new LED light over the nav-station after finding the fixture yesterday while digging through the compartments.

Oh, I must also mention I'm a grandfather, once again, as our daughter Heather just had a new baby boy that came a little early, weighing in at 6 lbs. 1 oz. The name is Breyden Lucas Thornton. Sounds like more crew for the future.

DAY 54

Current Stats
Position
Lat. 54°15'S / Long. 49°06'W
Weather
Barometer = 986 mb. -- Wind = 8-12 kts. - - Temp = 44°-49°
Seas
2-4 ft.
Distance
24 hr. run = 99 NM
Miles sailed last three days = 299 NM
Total miles sailed so far = 7027 NM
Miles left to go to Cape of Good Hope = 2450 NM
Top speed so far
12.2 kts.

Today, the winds seem to be light and on Christmas break. I have a card to open from Debbie, and I hope Santa swings by Antarctica, dropping off some fresh breezes that will allow me to get crashing along to where I'm going. I'm still undecided what will be on the menu for Christmas, but roast chicken might have to do.

DAY 55 - CHRISTMAS EVE

I was looking forward to a great Christmas Eve, as the winds were filling in and starting to build up the seas, meaning we could cover some ground towards home. It was about noon when I was inspecting the genoa and was disappointed to see three tears starting to open up. I pulled the genoa off the furler, which is not an easy job while running before 17 knots of wind, and one of the tears went from about 3 inches to 18 inches during the process of getting the sail off the furler. Once again, I find myself sliding around tethered off on the foredeck sewing on more patches. Fortunately, I was able to cover two of the small tears with one patch. My contact cement was no longer a liquid, so I had to resort to silicone to hold the patches in place on both sides while I stitched them together. After about 1 hour 30 minutes, I struggled to get the sail back up on the furler and trimmed in. When I was admiring my not so beautiful patches, I discovered three more tears. Once again, I pulled the sail off the furler and repeated the patching drill. Fortunately, the wind had died down a little this time, and it was much easier to get the sail back up and flying.

I have to tell you, the thumb on my right hand is killing me, as I have been doing so much hand sewing that it bleeds each time I do it, and the finger nail is cutting into my thumb. It doesn't get a chance to heal, and it seems I cannot do anything without using it or jamming it into something. By the time I got everything cleaned up and put away, I was pretty knocked out, and celebrating would have to come on Christmas morning.

DAY 56 - CHRISTMAS MORNING

Christmas morning started like a fire drill. The winds built to 40 knots, and I was anxious to get out there and roll in the little bit of genoa and drop the Mizzen sail altogether, trying to get the boat back under control, as it was ripping across the ocean, careening way over on her port side. At last, we were back sailing in a civilized manner, even in the powerful winds that had backed down to about 30 knots.

Once below, I started the coffee percolating and was getting things ready for a nice breakfast. Then, we were slammed by a rogue wave on the starboard side, and I watched as the coffee pot flew across the galley, spilling water and grounds everywhere. "Merry Christmas" and "Ho Ho Ho!" Here we go again, on a second attempt to make a pot of coffee. This time, it was watched much more closely, and like the last one, it was bungee corded down and had the fiddles sucked tight around the pot.

It was time to go outside and get the Spot locator device that is sending out our location. I pushed open the double companionway doors and suddenly felt I had entered the world of "Oz", as right before my eyes was a huge Iceberg over a mile and a half long and some 800 feet high. My knees shook as I gazed in disbelief, as we were already past it and could have just as easily T-boned the thing. It appeared to be about a mile away. Once I got the radar up and going after a bunch of filming and pictures, it was actually four miles away, but its enormous size made it seem much closer. The iceberg was very visible on the radar; even at 16 miles, I was still able to see it. It was with the radar that I could determine its size. Our track showed we had come within two miles of it when we passed. We had truly lucked out! I thought I was north of the icebergs, as the ones I have the locations on are 200 miles to the south of me, so from now on, the radar stays on 24/7. I can imagine, had we slammed into that iceberg at 7 knots, we probably would have not only peeled some paint off the bow-sprit, but it is possible we could have caused the iceberg to emit some CO_2 into the atmosphere, as I'm also sure there would have been a huge release of methane gas from the Sailors Run.

DAY 57

The winds today have dropped way down as we are sailing along very comfortably towards our destination, sometimes even under sunny skies. I have seen three ships since the Horn. Two of them were at the Horn and were small 90-meter passenger ships, the "Plancius" and the "Polar Princess" that both appeared to come up from Antarctica and went to the Horn for photos. The third ship, a much larger freighter by the name of "Britannia," was paralleling my course just to the south of me. Other than that traffic, all's been quiet in the South Atlantic.

DAY 58

This day finds us sailing along in the bright sunshine on a beam reach, and we have the fishing line out, as the freezer is empty. The temperature still seems very cool, partially because the wind is out of the south. I'm happy to report that, today, there are no new tears in the genoa.

DAY 59

We have finally arrived back up to the 48° latitude, and it seems about 5 degrees warmer, making life much more comfortable aboard. Now, all we have to do is sail due east around the world until we get within 400 miles of Chile then turn north for home. Well, it sounds all too simple but most likely not. I see another low-pressure system just ahead of us, but hopefully, we will miss the worst it has to offer.

DAY 60

It seems truly amazing that today is the end of my second month at sea, and this month seems to have passed twice as fast as last month.

The first of our three propane tanks is now empty. The replacement tank that has been tied on the rail seems light, like maybe only half full. The third tank is full, so we will see how this tank holds up. "No Coffee—come on!"

So far, we have caught no water as it has either been foggy or a light drizzle and no good, heavy rain. I might have to do a rain dance to get things pouring.

Just a tip on sailing in the Southern Ocean; don't let these not-so-cold temperatures fool you. When you are tying in reefs in 30-40 knots of wind and it is foggy or drizzling, you can only stand to do it for about ten minutes before you have to warm your hands. Before you head topside, you must have a clear picture in your mind what needs to be done to stabilize the boat quickly. Many times, several things must be done, and you might have to pull off to warm your hands.

Days 31-60

On day 60, we have encountered yet another deep low and find ourselves sailing along in gale force conditions. The winds are 30-35 knots, gusting 40+ knots. At first, the winds were from the north, and these lasted about 12 hours. Then, suddenly, we sail into the center of the low, and the winds drop to zero. This is the worst-case scenario, as you are bobbing around like a cork, and your sails are slamming and popping on the boom. I'm torn as to what to do. If I drop the sail, the rolling will be much worse, and if I leave it up, there could be damage. I make a cup of cocoa and try to drink it while my stomach is tied in knots over what to do. I go topside, grabbing for whatever will keep me in the cockpit. It's dark, and I try to get a read on what the wind will do next. At last, I decide to gybe, as it appears the wind is just starting to fill slightly from the south about 180° from where it had been coming. Soon, the main boom settled down, and I read two knots of speed on the G.P.S. We are starting to move once again. In the next 10 minutes, the wind increases to about 15 knots. I roll out a small portion of the genoa on the furler, getting our speed up over 5 knots. I go below, where I had been sleeping before all the slamming and banging started, and crawl back into my berth, hugging my Tequila bottle with hot water in it, trying to warm up. Soon, I'm asleep and stay that way for about an hour, but then I'm awakened by the sound of water rushing by the hull, and the boat is forced hard over on her side. I climb out of my berth and look at the G.P.S. speed and see we are doing from 8-10 knots, way too fast if you want to keep your rig in one piece. This is the fun part as the winds are over 30 knots once again, and I cannot get outside to do anything until I have on all my foul weather and safety gear. It's the fire drill and time to go full on. After a very long 5 minutes, I kind of stumble and dive out into the cockpit, grabbing for the sheet line to the genoa that must be released to furl in that vulnerable sail. This takes a couple of minutes, then I slack the main to further reduce strain on the rig. The next thing I do is adjust the wind-vane to steer more downwind on a reach running away from these powerful winds.

Once back below decks, it takes a few minutes to get the adrenaline turned off and, once again, hop back in my bunk with the Tequila bottle. The problem with the gale force conditions is that you always must put on all your foul weather gear before going outside. I mean, you can't go out for one minute without it for fear you will be drenched by a breaking wave and all your warm weather gear washed down with salt water. Once the salt water gets it, the stuff will not dry until washed, and then it will take days to dry.

Just trying to stay upright and dry, sailing along in the South Atlantic, the Jefe'.

Storm comes back on days 34-35.

Huge wave slips under our stern on day 35.

Fortunately, we arrive on the lee-shore of Chile in good weather.

The Jefe' with Cape Horn in the background on Day-48.

The skipper drinks a toast at Cape Horn.

The iceberg I missed by just two-miles, now seven miles distant.

Cold ass sailing down here.

Chapter 7: Days 61-80

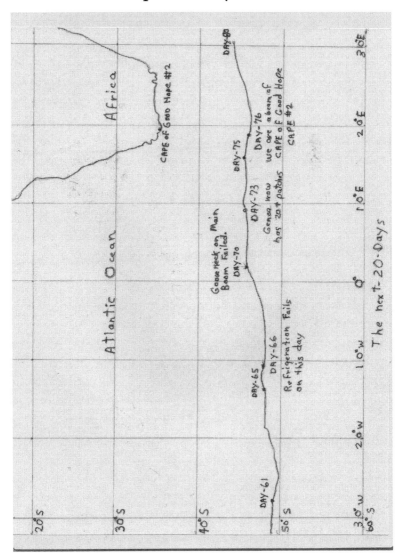

The next 20-Days

Atlantic Ocean

Africa

CAPE of Good Hope #2

DAY-80

DAY-75

DAY-76

we are abeam of
CAPE of Good Hope
CAPE #2

DAY-73

Genoa now
has torn patches

Goose neck on Main
Boom Failed.

DAY-70

DAY-65

DAY-66

Refrigeration Fails
on this day

DAY-61

20°S 30°S 40°S 50°S 60°S

3.0°W 2.0°W 1.0°W 0° 1.0°E 2.0°E 3.0°E

DAY 61

Today, the sun is out, and the winds have moderated. It never ceases to amaze me when I go out on deck and watch all the birds demonstrating their flying skills. Sometimes, there are as many as 20+ birds and usually three to five different varieties.

Today, while washing dishes, I happened to glance out the window and saw two birds floating up over a wave and was surprised when they took off underwater, as they were actually penguins. I guess they forage for food this far north from Antarctica or may have an iceberg parked someplace just over the horizon. I try fishing again but must pull in the line, as all the birds are attacking the rubber squid, actually tearing the thing apart and not even getting hooked.

Overnight, the winds go back up to gale force 35-40 knots, and I reduce sail to just the staysail and reefed main. Even with that, it still feels like a bit too much sail.

DAY 62 - NEW YEAR'S EVE

The day starts nice, sailing along in 25 knots. I have decided to stay home this year and avoid all the cops on the highway. The really cool thing about sailing the Southern Ocean is you can get sloshed every day without drinking anything, not to mention staggering when you try to walk; things are always getting spilled, and it's all free and just part of the experience.

I will be making some kind of tuna fish spaghetti, with garlic, tomato sauce, onions, and Italian seasoning. I hope it turns out OK.

Overnight, the winds crank up to gale force once again. I prop myself up on one elbow, so I can see the A.I.S., first to be sure there are no targets [ships], and then the speed, which was 7-9 knots, and the course, which was about 40-degrees off from what I wanted. But even with a gybe, I would still be twenty degrees off. The winds were forecast to shift favorably before too long, so I just curled back up with my "Hot Tequila" bottle and drifted off to sleep, awakening an hour later, pleased to see we were back on course. This morning, I awoke to a very cool cabin at 41 degrees Fahrenheit and was a little shocked when I looked topsides and found about one inch of slushy snow. It's summer down here with 19 hours of daylight, and that makes me hope I get out of here before it becomes winter. Oh well, I had a white Christmas thanks to the iceberg and now a white New Year's Day with snow.

DAY 63

Today looks like a good sailing day, and it should put us beyond the halfway point of crossing the Atlantic. I fell about 4 days behind schedule in the Pacific due to adverse weather. My hopes of making the Cape of Good Hope by the 7th are out the window, and it looks more like the 12th at the earliest. When nature is your motor, you just have to make the most of what you receive for power. There is another low that appears to be forming directly ahead of me. Although it is not intense, they are always like opening Pandora's box, full of unpredictability that jumps out at you.

Sailors Run, still bumping along on one cold ass ride, the Jefe'.

DAY 64

We are sailing in lighter airs now, so I let out more of the genoa only to discover yet another small tear. I immediately roll it back in and decide that I must wait for a good opportunity to pull the sail off the furler, once again, for repairs.

I'm awakened to the sound of the main boom bouncing against its restraints, as the winds have died down. It's 1 a.m. and already light outside. I climb out of my berth and heat up some left-over coffee, as the time has come to repair the genoa. I stagger about the cabin, getting the necessary materials together to make the repair. I drink the coffee, looking for that little burst of energy that comes from the caffeine and the thawing out of my fingers that are warmed by clinging to the hot cup in my hands. Once up on deck, I get the sail rolled all the way out. I go forward and release the halyard, dropping the sail as I struggle to tug it aboard, keeping it out of the ocean. Once the sail is on deck, I take a black marking pen and circle the tear and inspect the sail for other tears, finding three more. I go below and cut out the 8 patches needed to make the 4 repairs. Once again, I find myself tethered in on the foredeck, and I set about gluing the patches into place on both sides with silicone sealant. During this process, I discover two more tears, so more patches and more silicone. A squall comes along, and I'm pummeled by hail as I struggle to complete sewing the patches into place, normally a not so difficult job, but here in a hostile environment, it becomes much more challenging. By 6 a.m., the sail has 6 new patches, looking now more like a quilt that I once saw my grandmother making than a sail! I pull the sail back up in the aluminum track and fly it full out. It appears that I have little choice but to fly it all the way out or roll it all the way up in anything over 15 knots and rely on the rest of the sails to move us along in the heavier air.

DAY 65

I was out in the cockpit scanning the horizon, when I saw a whale blow off the starboard beam. The whale was some distance off, and I never did see it, but the geyser it put up was amazing. The winds seem to be going lighter now, and we are having frequent isolated squalls with snow and hail.

The Seattle Seahawks had a great game against the Arizona Cardinals, and I think, at one point in the game, I could even hear Debbie cheering clear down here.

One thing I notice down here is wrapping your fingers around a hot cup of coffee means almost as much as drinking it, and I know I like my "Tequila bottle" full of hot water more than any of the ones I have with Tequila in them.

DAY 66

Current Stats
Position
Lat. 48°07'S / Long. 10°48'W
Weather
Barometer = 1013 mb. -- Wind = 12-30 kts. - - Temp = 42°-47°
Seas
6-12 ft.
Distance
24 hr. run = 161 NM
Miles sailed last three days = 421 NM
Total miles sailed so far = 8748 NM
Miles left to go to Cape of Good Hope = 1160 NM
Top speed so far
12.2 kts.

I watch in amazement at the birds that continually soar around the boat. I can't help but think about how getting older and ailments like arthritis can have such an effect on human beings, and then imagine the effects on a bird that needs to be in constant flight to survive.

I'm not sure what all can go wrong on the Sailors Run on a voyage of this duration, but I'm pretty sure we are in record territory, as the refrigeration has just gone "tits up". The good news is, there is no meat in the freezer, and the whole boat is just about at refrigeration temperature near 42°, most of the time anyhow. That ice machine that I was regretting dragging along might come in handy when I hit warmer temperatures.

There are some gale force winds coming my way and will be with us for several days, so I'm checking the old Sailors Run, getting her ready for the wild ride that is on its way. These winds are predicted to be 35 knots with higher gusts. The good thing is they will be west or NW winds and, hopefully, warmer than the southerlies we have been having.

The Jefe'

"Battening down the hatches", the Jefe'.

DAY 67

Today, we awaken to a "kick ass" ride in heavy winds and large
seas. The winds came upon us in the early hours of the morning, and the seas became treacherous about 6 hours later. Near
mid-morning, I began to hear the staysail luffing badly out on
deck. Once in my foulies and boots, I went topside to see what
the hell was going on. It suddenly was obvious the wire staysail
pendant that holds the tack of the sail down to the bowsprit
had failed. The sail was luffing wildly, sliding up and down on
the staysail shroud, making one heck of a racket. I grabbed a
piece of half-inch line and made a pendant out of that and secured the tack of the sail, once again, an easy fix.

It had become obvious to me that Sailors Run had become
over-powered. I put a second reef in the main and felt confident that, with this and only the staysail up, we were ready for
the weather that was forecasted to be in our area. In the early
afternoon, while I was reading below deck, the boat suddenly
turned up into the wind, indicating a steering problem. I
scrambled as fast as I could to get into my foul weather gear
and get out on deck. Things were deteriorating rapidly, and it
was now blowing a full gale with ever-increasing wave heights.
The first things to catch my eye were the slack steering lines
coming to the wheel from the Monitor wind vane. After a little
closer scrutiny, the problem was obvious—the stopper knot on
the end of the line had parted, where it connected to the servo
rudder on the wind vane. Of course, the line had pulled back
up inside the pulley and tube, which required getting some
slack out of the extra line where it attaches to the wheel lines
and fishing it back out of the tube and around the pulley. At
anchor, this would be simple, but in a gale, hanging by your
toes over the back of the boat in frigid waters that always seem
to find their way up to your arm pits, this is no easy task. Soon,
I have the knot retied on the line, and I disconnect the elec-

tronic pilot that has been steering as I made the repairs—just one more reason to have redundancy in steering systems.

The winds are now blowing 35-45 knots and the seas running twenty feet or more, making getting any sleep below difficult. At last, I manage to drift off when, once again, Sailors Run is slammed by a steep breaking wave, and water sprays below through the seals on the overhead butterfly hatch. I'm torn from a deep sleep and must spring into action, ripping the pillow case from my pillow, trying to keep the pillow as dry as possible and getting the saturated portions of the blankets to hang outside the "lee cloth," keeping the rest of the bedding dry. Thank God it was only spray that got in.

DAY 68

Another new day dawns, and the winds have abated to 25 knots, and the seas are starting to come down. I go forward to shake one of the reefs out of the main, and I'm disappointed at what I discover. The brand new main has three slides that are so thin and inferior that they bent and pulled out of the mast track! I make a mental note that, if I live through this adventure, Lee Sails will hear about this. I had noticed when putting on the new main in Ecuador that the slides on this new mainsail were half as thick as the ones on the new mizzen; that sail is half the size, and it has given me no trouble thus far.

While I'm considering what to replace these bad slides with, I make another startling discovery that sends a wave of chilling concern through me. The new gooseneck I had manufactured in Mexico has several cracks in the plates that attach it to the pivot bolt on which it swings, and I know there is no easy fix for this one. I brainstorm for several hours on how to reinforce the gooseneck, but in the end, I decide all I can do is baby it and hope it will hold together.

I also determine, if it should fail, I could end up taking the boom in the nuts, a most likely scenario the way my luck has been running. I could just fly the main loose-footed for the rest of the voyage. I'm feeling a little better knowing this is not a total threat to the success of the voyage but just another handicap with which we will be forced to operate.

DAY 69

Today finds us running before building seas in westerly winds at 35-50 knots, and under staysail alone, we are still seeing speeds up to 10 knots. These seas are large and tend to toss us about, first coming in on one side then the other. What has happened is a large high-pressure system, rotating counter-clockwise here in the southern hemisphere, is north of us and intensifying as it moves down over us. The good thing is we are "rocketing along" on course.

DAY 70

Tomorrow will be a special day as we cross the 000-degree longitude Meridian, and we will actually be on true Zulu time.

I was awakened at three a.m. when I heard the mainsail banging around in very light winds. I went topside to see what I could do to quiet things down and save wear and tear on that weakened goose-neck fitting. I also noticed the boom seemed to be rolling back and forth excessively. I approached the main mast with apprehension, as I feared the gooseneck fitting had failed, and sure enough, it was half-broken and needed to be removed, while wind and sea conditions remained light.

It was a slow process working the boom free of the foot of the sail, but soon, the boom was tied on the cabin top, and I started jury-rigging the main to be free flown. First, you must realize, this sail is not cut to be flown like a jib and tends to bag out in the middle when slacked out, almost like a spinnaker. I discovered the only way this was going to work was to tie in the first reef and hang a single block in the clew of the first row of reef points. Fortunately, being a ketch, my mast is a little further forward, and the mainsheet traveler runs on the cabin top just in front of the dodger. This setup, although less than desirable for good performance, was extremely easy to drop out when a blow suddenly comes upon us. The free flying main was least efficient in light air going to weather.

DAY 71

I continue to struggle with the new Lee mainsail, as two more slides have pulled out of the track and must be replaced. With the main now flying loose-footed, I roll out the genoa to go to weather in the light air and am not surprised to see yet another tear about 4 inches Long. I roll the tear onto the foil, as I'm just too tired from getting the main converted. Now, if all this is not just about enough, I see the worst storm that I have yet had to deal with coming my way. It's a very intense low-pressure that will be packing winds sustained over 50 knots, gusting to 65 knots. We hope to be on the upper shoulder of this storm, with it passing south of us, and there will be 35-foot seas in the dangerous quadrant that I'm hoping to avoid as I alter course to go more to the north.

DAY 72

I pulled the genoa off the furler yesterday and installed six patches on the genoa then decided to take it below and rework the 5mm luff cord that needed to be re-sewn to the luff of the sail in three areas. I keep the sail below as all hell is starting to break loose up on deck. The main is dropped clear out, and we are under staysail alone, heading into the night. Still more trouble, I discover the double mainsheet block is now failing and is no longer usable without major repairs. It's now blowing over 30 knots, and I feel as exhausted as I have yet to be on this trip. I hope to be able to get some sleep sometime during the course of this night.

"Three wheels" on my wagon, and I'm still sailing along!

DAY 73

Sailed along nicely all day in 30 knots of breeze with just the staysail. I'm waiting for the winds to die down a bit before re-rigging in order to free-fly the mainsail. I awaken about 11 p.m. and see it is just beginning to get light outside. I also see our speed has dropped below 5 knots, and it's time to get the main back up. Once up on deck, I remove the block that I use for my sea anchor and shackle it to the clew of the sail. I fit a new bolt into my double mainsheet block, repairing it, then run the main sheet line through the main sheet block up to the block on the clew of the sail and back down to the becket on the main sheet block, giving me a two to one purchase and distributing the load over the main sheet block. I put the main back up, and it looks great, and I feel that this set-up will get us home.

Just a little clarification on all the sail issues we are having:

A. The mainsail is brand new, but Lee sails installed the wrong slides that go in the mast, and they are pulling out in strong winds. I have had to replace four of them that have failed and now feel pretty confident there will be no more issues with the main.

B. The mizzen sail is brand new, and I have had no problems with it.

C. The staysail is in brand new condition with no problems.

D. The "Genoa from Hell" is only 5 years old, and I have totally overestimated its condition and ability to make this voyage. It obviously is suffering from UV-damage [the sun] and can't be flown partially rolled out. I also believe sometimes it is damaged when being furled in when winds begin to increase. It is sporting over 20 patches.

DAY 74

Today is truly a great sailing day, and the sun is out. I have had no luck catching rainwater, as it seems it only rains when it is blowing 25+ knots, and catching water on deck is made impossible by saltwater flying everywhere. I'm conserving water everywhere I can, and that means showering less frequently. Now, you must envision what a balancing act it is to try taking a shower on this roller coaster, not to mention it being a bone-chilling adventure. I have decided to build a water distiller, and I actually have the time to do it.

DAY 75

Current Stats

Position
Lat. 45°18'S / Long. 16°15'E

Weather
Barometer = 1003 mb. -- Wind = 20-40 kts. - - Temp = 48°-55°

Seas
8-15 ft.

Distance
24 hr. run = 136 NM
Miles sailed last three days = 422 NM
Total miles sailed so far = 9979 NM
Miles left to go to Cape of Good Hope = 92 NM

Top speed so far
12.3 kts.

Today, if I were having the circumnavigation of my dreams, I would already be halfway there. That is just not the case, and it will be interesting to see when I do reach the midpoint, mileage-wise. Who knows? Maybe the second half will go faster.

I took two hours and built a water distiller, and tomorrow, I will bring it online and see if it works. I used two 5-gallon gas jugs that I normally only use for water storage. One 5-gallon jug will hold the salt water, and it will be wrapped in a black plastic bag, hoping to create some heat; the other one will be the condenser unit that will feed water into a half-gallon container, and this will all be lashed out in the cockpit. I'm hoping this will work.

It was late afternoon when a cold front hit us, coming in from the southwest, and I was forced to drop the main, as the winds are gusting to 40 knots. The seas are becoming very confused with the sudden wind shift to the south, and the storm-force seas coming up from the south are rapidly building into dangerously steep seas. Occasionally, a wave manages to come in on our beam, and it is like being slammed by a freight train. I watch as torrents of water rush along our decks as Sailors Run valiantly shakes free of these pummeling blows to rise once again to be less of a submarine. It is very uncomfortable below decks as we are now cork-screwing along. It is so frustrating, as the winds are now from a perfect direction to sail our desired course line, yet I have to sail NE to keep Sailors Run's stern into the punishing waves, thereby avoiding a catastrophic roll over.

"How dry I am, how dry I am, nobody knows how dry I am."

Looking for water along the route—the Jefe'.

DAY 76

Today marks another milestone for the Sailors Run, as after over 10,000 NM, 75 days and 21 hours, the Cape of Good Hope is abeam. Of course, even though it is 4 a.m., a toast of one shot of 12-year-old Cuban Rum is enjoyed. This is the second great cape, a major milestone of the journey. I find myself pretty emotional as I venture for the first time into the Indian Ocean. I greatly appreciate my lovely wife Debbie and all our family and friends for hanging in there with me, not to mention all the prayers from the many friends that are following along.

Now, it's on into the Indian Ocean and another 3,900 NM to our third southern cape, Cape Leeuwin, Australia. I'm sure some of you have wondered if I ever thought of packing it all in and sailing for home—well, the answer is an emphatic NO! I have never been good at quitting a challenge that I have undertaken. Believe me, I know what it feels like to want to quit, having run several marathons in under 3 hours. For me, as long as I can see the remotest chance of success, I keep going. It occurred to me today that I'm experiencing a strange phenomenon; I believe this is the first time I have set out on a voyage and will not have to turn around to come back. Think about it!

DAY 77

Today, in the lighter morning breeze, I was able to put the genoa back up on the furler. I sailed with it through the daytime hours, eventually having to roll it in as winds increased.

Bruce Schwab has cautioned me that the most treacherous sailing conditions he ever experienced were in the Southern Indian Ocean. Bruce is a Two-Time World Circumnavigator, who soloed "Ocean Planet" in two Around Alone Races. So now, I get to see if I will have a similar experience.

Last night, I cut up one of my giant squash. I cubed some of it and cooked it. The squash was great, and now, I just hope it will keep until I can get it all eaten. That sucker must have weighed 15 lbs.

DAY 78

Now, I must be honest with you and say my new "Desert Dry Water Distiller" for offshore cruisers is living up to its name. After several days, I have yet to see a drop of water in the production water container. It might be a case where you must cut the condenser jug into slabs of plastic and lick the inside area to obtain any water. Oh well—it was an idea.

I should mention that another experiment has been quite successful. 83 days ago, I purchased 4 loaves of the cheapest wheat bread I could buy, with the idea that it would have lots of preservatives in it and therefore would keep well. I can hon-

The Jefe'

estly say I can still make a tuna sandwich, and the bread is soft and tastes fresh and no mold. I don't know how long the bread can keep doing this, but I still have 2.5 loaves left and will most likely find out.

To conserve water, I'm now washing the dishes in salt water with a little fresh water rinse.

Looking for rain, your Amigo, the Jefe'.

DAY 79

Today, I actually had some rain, with light winds, so I was able to collect about 6 gallons into the empty second tank. That's a start!

The more challenging thing right now is trying to stay hooked up to Sailmail. Chile has been a great station but is now over 3500 miles away, and the signal is becoming too weak. The next station is in Australia, at least another 3500+ miles away and is way too weak at this time. I assumed I would be able to use the Africa station but have come to find out they use a directional antenna. Unfortunately, it is facing NE, not down into the Southern Ocean, and unable to reach my current location. Debbie has been alerted that I have a radio problem and follows me on the Spot Locator, but that is all she has to go on. This is a huge problem for me, as I get most of my weather info from Sailmail. For now, I will have to get my weather from the barometer and looking out the port hole.

DAY 80

The night before last, a high-pressure system was located on top of me, causing shifting winds. At one point, I awoke to discover I was headed back to the Cape of Good Hope. Fortunately, it had only been about two hours, and with the winds light, we were moving slowly.

Here in the Southern Indian Ocean, I have seen some of the largest albatross so far, some with wing spans that must be

7-8 feet. It never ceases to amaze me how well they can fly in the heavy winds.

I have been truly enjoying my Kindle for making lots of books available and being so user friendly.

I have been struggling with the time change, as the further East I go, the earlier it gets light. Now, based on Ecuador time, the sun is rising at 9 p.m. and sets at about 1 p.m. I find myself just taking two-hour naps whenever I feel like I need it. I run the Radar and AIS 24/7 and have seen no ships since the vicinity of Cape Horn. The last thing I saw was the "Ice Berg" that I almost collided with.

Failed goose neck, boom down on deck indefinitely.

Mainsail configuration for the remaining 19,000 nautical miles.

Running bare poles in 50kts. of wind.

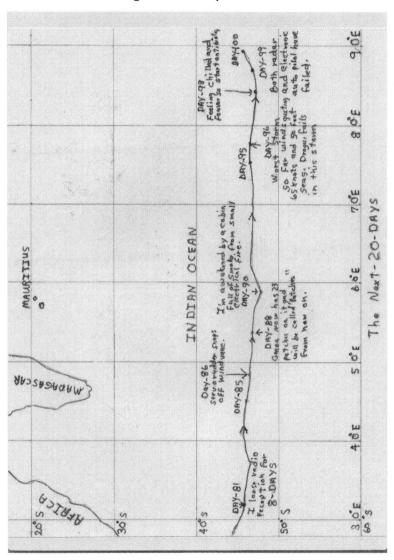

The Next 20 DAYS

INDIAN OCEAN

AFRICA

MADAGASCAR

MAURITIUS

DAY-81
I loose radio reception for 8-DAYS

DAY-85

DAY-86
Servo-rudder snaps off windvane.

DAY-88
Oman now has 23 patches on it and will be called "Patches" from now on.

DAY-90
I'm awakened by a cabin full of smoke from small electrical fire.

DAY-95

DAY-96
Worst storm. So far winds gusting and electronic 65 knots and 50 feet auto pilot have seas; Drogue fails failed. in this storm

DAY-98
Feeling chipped and paranoia starts setting in

DAY-99
Both radar

DAY-100

The Jefe'

DAY 81

Today was one of those days where many sail changes had to be made, and in the end, we were under staysail alone in 35+ knots.

It feels strange to have no communication, but I know that, within a week or two, I should be able to get back online. I still have the Spot locator, and that lets some people know my current location. It also allows me to let Debbie know I have lost radio communication. Once I get a good Sailmail signal, I will get out the backlog of adventures, so my followers can catch up on what has been going on.

I'm looking for the big "Radio Skip" in the Southern Ocean. —"Breaker Breaker", the Jefe'.

DAY 82

Wow!! 82 days totally alone, not another soul to lay eyes upon. This all seems pretty strange. I'm definitely a prisoner of this voyage, and thank God, it is by my own doing. I must admit the sunny days are my favorite as it is warmer, and it makes the ocean that we are sailing upon look so much more beautiful.

The radio is still not hooking up to Sailmail, and I just hope friends and family understand; things are fine aboard Sailors Run. I search the radio for news, but all I get is African news, and that is a whole new level of depressing info.

DAY 83

Today, we sailed over the top of Prince Edward Islands about 90 miles to the south of us; there are only two Islands there, and they are quite small. It appears I'm about 4 days from the half-way point of my circumnavigation, at least mileage-wise. I'm sailing as hard and fast as I can with the vulnerable genoa sail, which I only fly all the way out in winds of less than 17 knots.

The weather has not been very severe the last few days, "knock on wood" [my head]. The boat is going to need lots of TLC once we make Bahía Caraquez, Ecuador.

DAY 84

It seems I'm finding a rhythm with the Southern Ocean. I had originally planned to sail across the Atlantic and Indian Oceans at 48°S latitude, but it seems to be more productive at 45°S latitude. The winds and cold fronts seem less violent, and the temperature is about 10-degrees warmer.

Yet another system of when to add or reduce sail has evolved. I now use the 30-minute rule when I think a sail change is needed, because if I don't wait, 50% of the time, the choice is wrong. Of course, if you are pounced upon by a huge squall, there is no waiting to reduce the sail and take the load off the rig.

DAY 85

During this day, I watched the barometer plummet from 998 to 992 then rebound to 1004 mb, all within 24 hours. The winds became very strong when they switched from NW to SW, and once again, we sailed along under staysail alone with winds gusting 40 knots for about 13 hours. Sailing in the Southern Ocean requires staying on top of the ever-changing environment. A typical day aboard Sailors Run involves four to eight sail changes. The reason so many are necessary is the rapidly changing strength of the wind, often varying from 10-40+ knots.

The weather here in the "Roaring-Forties" brings a deep low to your area every two to three days and normally gale force winds or worse.

DAY 86

Today, the low that we have been sailing in has deepened and appears to be moving over the top of us, as the winds are now

The Jefe'

30 knots. Sailors Run has just turned up into the wind, and yet another apparent steering problem has come up. I scramble to put on my foulies and get out into the cockpit. It is immediately obvious what is wrong, as once again, we have that silver looking salmon dragging along behind the boat, which, in reality, is the servo-rudder of the wind vane. I put the boat on the electronic autopilot and go below to manufacture a new tube section to get the wind vane going again. The wind vane does an amazing amount of work steering the boat and is perhaps the most valuable addition ever put on Sailors Run. Thank God I got the wind vane fixed when I did, as now, the barometer continues to fall and is reading 984 mb. The winds are blowing 45 knots, gusting 55 knots, and the seas are running 20-30 ft. I'm forced to sail more south than east to keep these huge waves on my stern. Before I turned more south, Sailors Run was being slammed on the side every 20 minutes by breaking waves, and some water was finding its way below. Now that they are on our stern, the only thing that happens is the cockpit is filled on a regular basis.

This gale/storm is one of the worst I have seen so far. The storm was intense for about 18 hours, then the center passed over me. After about 1-1/2 hours, I entered and rode out the backside of the system. A storm such as this brings an amazing amount of rugged beauty to those that dare come this way. It is filled with all the colors of the sea, the white foam of the breakers cascading down the face of huge and very steep waves. Although frightening as it may be, it also makes you feel so totally alive. You find yourself mesmerized for hours just staring out at these amazing forces of nature in action.

DAY 87

Current Stats

Position
Lat. 45°44'S / Long. 51°16'E

Weather
Barometer = 1010 mb. -- Wind = 8-35 kts. - - Temp = 46°-55°

Seas
15-20 ft.

Distance
24 hr. run = 115 NM
Miles sailed last three days = 404 NM
Total miles sailed so far = 11,586 NM
Miles left to go to Cape Leeuwin = 2640 NM

Top speed so far
12.3 kts.

Today is a very special day, as we have arrived at what I believe to be the half-way point of our circumnavigation!! Yea!! Well, at least mileage-wise I believe this to be half-way; time-wise could be different, as no two days of sailing are the same. All things considered, this should put me across the finish line at Bahía Caraquez, Ecuador on or about the 22nd of April 2016. I will have also celebrated my 70th birthday on the 17th of April. Of course, the real party will be in Bahía with Debbie and friends.

I am now sailing just 28 miles north of the Crozet Islands—a small group of islands made up of three primary islands that each appear to be 5-10 miles in length. One can be pretty sure they are a huge nesting area for thousands of sea birds, as the skies around Sailor Run are now filled with hundreds of birds, many of them large albatross.

Aging along the way, the Jefe'.

The Jefe'

Today was a busy and mysterious day. After breakfast, I looked into a problem I was having getting the autopilot to engage into the quadrant below decks. Of course, that involves pulling out lots of gear to get at it, including the 60 lb. CQR anchor. The fix was easy. The Morse cable had slipped where it was clamped down and just needed adjustment and tightening. It is very important to have a backup to the wind vane, because when you must work on the wind vane and there is no other person aboard to do the steering, it could be a big problem.

A high is moving over us, and once again, the winds are going light, so I roll out the genoa now known as "Patches" and see yet another tear in it! I pull the sail off the furler and look it over. Once down on deck, I find a total of three tears that require patches. Fortunately, today the winds are light, and the seas are down with bright sunshine.

Things became disturbingly mysterious as I was sewing on the last patch. I started hearing what sounded like muffled explosions off in the distance and a rumbling that went on continuously for several minutes. I scanned the horizon looking for thunderclouds, but there was only blue sky. I searched the sky for a jet plane, and there was nothing to be seen then the surface of the sea for a ship, still nothing. My mind tells me it was either a volcanic eruption under the sea, although I have seen no steam, or possibly an earthquake. The truth is I don't know what it was.

Now getting back to the genoa—"Patches". I have composed a song for it, and it goes like this.

Patches oh, what should I do?
I swear I'll always fix you.
Though it may not be right,
I'm coming for you tonight.
Patches, I'll always need you.

Days 81-100
[See—you can go nuts out here!]

DAY 89

Today, we sailed in light air that started slowly building overnight from the north.

I can't begin to tell you how confusing it is when it gets light about 20 minutes earlier every day. When you are on a Bahía time schedule, it just seems really strange to wake up in the morning when it gets light and realize it's 9pm.

The food supplies are holding up well with the exception of the Coke that is now zero, and there are but six onions and one apple left. I still have a lot of food in cans etc., yet I truly messed up by not buying a lot of popcorn. I love it but was afraid I might break a tooth eating it. Oh well, next time: more popcorn!

At last, Sailmail finally hooked up on the African station, "yahoo!" I now hope to keep radio communication going the rest of the way around. This is very important, not only to feel connected, but I also need that most valuable weather information. The GRIB files, pressure gradient faxes, along with satellite pictures of the ocean that surrounds me are instrumental in avoiding trouble and staying safe.

DAY 90

Stronger north winds to 40+ knots are coming today and will be on our beam.

I want to thank the "gang" at Latitude38.com for coming along on this voyage and keeping the readers updated as to our progress via that great magazine out of San Francisco, California.

It's funny how things work out, like the effects of the failure of the wind generator were canceled out by the failure of the refrigeration, so maybe two wrongs can make a right. The three solar panels keep up with all our electrical needs, like radar, A.I.S., electric autopilot when needed, lights, vhf radio, single side band radio, computers etc. I have been impressed by how well they have done, especially the two solar panels that are hung on the one-inch life-line rail on either side of the cockpit. Twice they have been knocked loose of one of their supporting legs. This was easily remedied by putting the stainless-steel leg back in the socket, which is mounted on the cap rail then tightening the Allen screw that attempts to keep them in place.

Last night, like always, I looked forward to crawling into my berth and getting some rest, one of my most favorite times of the day. I had been asleep for about 15 minutes when I smelled something burning. I opened my eyes and the cabin was pitch black—normally, the A.I.S. illuminates it with a soft light. I jumped out of my berth and turned on the light. The entire cabin was filled with smoke from an electrical fire. Fortunately, I smelled it when I did, as the air that I had been breathing was awful. I opened up the hatch and aired out the cabin, all the time coughing my lungs out.

Luckily, the breaker had tripped, and there was no ongoing fire. In the darkness, I was able to reset the breaker and saw where the wire shorted out. It was in the back of a small compartment, glowing and creating more of the acrid smoke. As it turned out, this was a 12-volt wire that we no longer used, and for some reason, the connection on the end of it had shorted out. It melted down to where I could not even recognize what it might have once been plugged into.

Attempting to suck up some fresher air in the Southern Ocean, the Jefe'.

DAY 91

Yesterday's blow continues at a sustained 40 knots, gusting 50 knots. These winds are caused by what is called a squash zone. We are caught between the high-pressure area, rotating counter-clockwise, and the low-pressure area, rotating clockwise, and where they push into each other, the isobars become compressed, causing the strong winds. It was about noon when suddenly the winds died from gusts of 50 to about 6 knots. Things immediately became chaotic aboard Sailors Run, as she began to roll gunnel to gunnel in the twenty-foot seas, with just a staysail up. I put up the main to reduce the rolling and soon regretted my decision, as the popping and banging of the sail appeared to be threatening the rig and sail. I took it for about 15 minutes then put my foulies back on and went topside to drop the main. I no more than got out in the cockpit and the wind started to fill in, settling the sails once again.

I'm currently attempting to sail further to the north in the direction of the forty-five-degree South latitude, as the last twenty hours of severe winds had forced us down near the forty-eight-degree latitude once again.

DAY 92

One might wonder why our mileage doesn't go up with the high winds.

There are several reasons:

1. You are sailing up and down over the huge waves and not on a flat-line course, forcing you to go further to get your mileage.

2. You must err on the side of caution with just how much sail you have up. And in my case, with no boom, I can't go to the second reef in the main, so it must come down in over thirty knots.

3. The other problem is "Patches" [the genoa]; normally in heavy wind, I would run the staysail with the genoa rolled out about 15-25%. This works great and keeps the sail area forward, making sailing off the wind easy to steer, but if I roll out Patches, she would just start disintegrating on me immediately. This is very frustrating, as it adds days to the voyage and the time it will take me to get back to Debbie.

DAY 93

The sailing today was great, and these are my thoughts from the Southern Ocean: To sail into the Southern Ocean with all its fury and remoteness requires a great amount of expertise in many areas, assuming we first remove stupidity as an area of expertise. Circumnavigating in that same ocean will test the mettle of even the best sailor.

One must come to grips with the all too real possibility that the loss of one's beloved vessel or even one's life is in the realm of possibilities. Every emotion known to man shall be experienced, as you travel along a very remote route, far from assistance and loved ones, in a most hostile environment. Here in the Southern Ocean, you are just a visitor, which becomes engulfed in all that nature sends your way. There are times you will feel sheer exhilaration, and others times, you will question the entire odyssey.

For me, most days pass rapidly as I live my sailing life with passion, yet other days leave me bored and questioning why I ever came. You see, down here, there are few distractions to the thoughts that might surface in your mind. Some of these lingering thoughts might be about the iceberg that you nearly collided with that could have ended your life here on earth as you know it. Or possibly you ponder, what if the mast goes over the side as your rig moans and groans under the tremendous pressure of a 50-knot blow, and your mind immediately starts to work through the scenario. Finally, you ask yourself, why fight ghosts that have yet to appear? My reasoning brings me to believe that, the longer you are in such a hostile environment, the greater the odds that one of your greatest fears might find you.

"Beating Feet" for the next cape, the Jefe'.

DAY 94

Today, we find Sailors Run sailing over the top of the Island Kerguelen, about 130 NM to the south of us. Kerguelen is a

French possession and geographically a very interesting Island because of all the amazing waterways and anchorages all around it. The Island is very large— approximately 70 miles by 60 miles, making it much larger than Hawaii. It is volcanic and popped up out of the ocean 35 million years ago, shortly before I got my first boat. The Island has a very harsh environment, with snow and glaciers, as well as winds that are clocked at 105 knots regularly every year. Mostly scientists and a few tourists visit each year. The sailing has been good the last three days, but another low will arrive tomorrow. Also, on this day, the cargo ship Tokyo Bunker passed 18 miles north of me bound for Australia.

DAY 95

Today, a gale approaches, so I drop the main and hoist a double-reefed mizzen and run the staysail. We are now sailing pretty well in 30 knots. I replaced a chafed line on the wind vane, and when I went to use the electronic autopilot, it didn't seem to want to work. It appears that it is jammed and kicks its breaker like it does when it is hard over and can't steer. I will have Debbie call on this one and see what she can find out. Later in the day, I popped my last popcorn and enjoyed it very much. I was kicking myself for not bringing more, as my crackers are also almost gone. Then I decided to take one more look in the popcorn locker, and there at the very bottom, I discovered 5 more bags 'Yahoo'!

As evening came on, so did the storm, and this one is rapidly intensifying and is much worse than predicted. I got soaked getting down the mizzen and staysail so I could run under bare poles once again.

DAY 96

Current Stats
Position
Lat. 46°51'S / Long. 77°41'E

Weather
Barometer = 990 mb. -- Wind = 50-65 kts. - - Temp = 48°-55°

Seas
20-40 ft.

Distance
24 hr. run = 143 NM
Miles sailed last three days = 433 NM
Total miles sailed so far = 12,820 NM
Miles left to go to Cape Leeuwin = 1500 NM

Top speed so far
14.1 kts.

The storm rages on with sustained winds of 50+ knots and gusting 65 knots. I have gone to the drogue[xii], as I was hitting 9 knots under bare poles. The drogue, a 6-foot delta, slowed the boat to about 3-4 knots and made things seem a little more under control. One large breaking wave took away my man-overboard-pole. Fortunately, it had no name on it, so if found, people won't be looking for me! Another breaking wave tore one of the struts off the solar panels, so I improvised another one out of schedule-40-PVC. This is, by far, the worst storm I have ever encountered at sea. The waves are getting monstrous at 40+ feet, and the wind is screeching and howling. I pray it will let up soon. I see a slight rise in the barometer and eagerly hope it keeps moving up.

Hanging in there in the "Big One", The Jefe'.

DAY 97 – THE STORM RECAP

First, let me say, I never saw this one coming, as it just appeared to be another 30-35 knot day. In reality, the 35 knots was just the beginning of a 48-hour battle for survival. Once I had set up the staysail and mizzen, I figured we were ready to handle what was to come our way. *Wrong!* I became suspicious when I noticed the barometer plummeting. The waves were also gradually growing larger, and one of these waves catapulted Sailors Run ahead at 14.1 knots. I knew the mizzen must come down. Once out on deck, it was obvious the staysail also must be eliminated, we would continue along under bare poles alone. It was while I was lashing the staysail on deck that a huge wave broke over the deck. As I hung on, I was thoroughly drenched to the core by this one; this would mandate a complete change of clothing. We sailed under bare poles for 16.5 hours, and by this time, we were seeing gusts to 65 knots and sustained winds in the 50+ knot range. The waves were becoming monstrous and the top 10 feet were breaking off and rolling down the face of some of them. At one point during the day, I looked out upon the sea and swore I was in the mountains, as it appeared there were snow covered peaks everywhere, with avalanches plummeting down their steep faces. We had been fairly successful in keeping our stern to the waves, but there are always a few rogue waves that will come in on your beam. One such wave took out one of my solar panel support struts, tearing the bracket from the cap rail. It was while I was replacing that support that a huge breaking wave closed in on the stern of Sailors Run. I looked up from my task at hand and remember thinking, "Oh My God" as I viewed the sun through this Coke-bottle blue wave, when suddenly its frothing, raging crest came charging down upon me and Sailors Run. I grabbed a lifeline stanchion and a nearby shroud and just hung on with all the strength left in me, only to be drenched to the bone for the second time this day.

During the storm, Sailors Run was engulfed by more than a dozen large waves. One such wave took away our man-overboard-pole[xiii]. Another one came in over the stern, not only filling the cockpit, but forcing green water through the louvers on the companionway doors, then hit the two storm boards I had in place and came up over the top like a waterfall cascading down into the galley. This left 10 gallons of water sloshing all over the cabin sole until I could get it bailed out. The waterfall also bathed our waterproof radar unit that has now stopped working. This is yet another big loss of an important piece of safety equipment, one more victim of a "vicious" Southern Ocean storm.

It was 2:30 p.m. when I deployed our Delta drogue on 400 feet of 5/8-inch nylon rode to slow the boat, as we were surfing bare poles at over 9 knots. This slowed us to 3-4 knots and made things feel more under control. We stayed on the drogue for 15 hours. It was the next morning when I pulled in the line to find the drogue had failed. All three of the factory nylon straps that attached it to the swivel had parted, and it was gone. I believe I know when it happened; I was writing Debbie when we were catapulted ahead by yet another huge wave. I saw the speed jump up to 9.1 knots and then noticed several other high speeds shortly thereafter. The total duration of the storm was about 48 hours. I truly hope not to encounter another storm like that one anytime soon. Over the next few days, I hope to get further north for better weather, if that's possible.

I must agree with ocean racer Bruce Schwab that the Indian Ocean seems to be a very *menacing* one.

DAY 98

Today, we are sailing through many squalls, hoping to get north. It is kind of a lick-your-wounds day. I woke up with a sore gland in my neck and felt chilled, so I started antibiotics, as I cannot afford to become sick in this hostile environment so far from help. I believe I have captured some great film and shots of the voyage and plan to produce a video, although I'm not sure what to sell it for until I assess the final damages to Sailors Run. It would seem the price is definitely on the rise!

DAY 99

Today, we are working through many squalls and making some progress to the north. We are still experiencing 20-foot waves. They refuse to lay down with the squalls continuing to breathe life back into them. The really big waves took about 18 hours to quit breaking and then at last started to subside. It seemed all too amazing to me that, while running "bare poles" and towing a drogue, we still managed to cover 117 NM. The gland in my neck is still sore, and I feel very sensitive to the cold. I'm pretty sure in a couple of days I will be fine.

Getting a little more religious as we go, The Jefe'.

DAY 100

It's amazing when you do battle with nature how fast she takes away your electrical and mechanical advantages, and it comes down to you, the boat, and your will to survive. It also seems amazing to me that we have been at sea now for "100 days". Today, I dropped the main, sailing under staysail alone in 25-35 knots. I pulled off the radar screen and opened it, looking for an obvious problem, only to find that the silicone rubber key pad seal was cracked and allowed storm wave water to breech the seal. Mystery solved, and all the time, I was thinking it was the fault of my indoor waterfall. I loved this radar unit, as it was small, required little power to run, and had operated perfectly for over twenty years. I will have another one of these radar units if we get through all that is set before us.

Severe breaking waves in worst storm so far; 65kt wind gusts.

Drogue after storm; no match for 65kt winds and 50-foot seas.

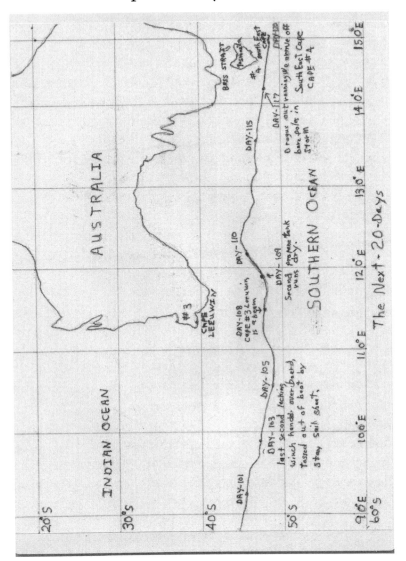

DAY 101

With many squalls now in my area, I am sailing with only a double-reefed mizzen and staysail. I worked over the wind vane, changing out a servo rudder line that was showing signs of chafe. I also tightened the two bolts at the bottom supports on the vane, as they were working loose. These two bolts receive a lot of torque and tend to become loose on a regular basis and should be checked every ten days or so when sailing in extreme conditions. Next, I dug back into the drive unit on the autopilot and re-soldered the three butt connection splices, hoping to get it up and running, but "no joy." I then pulled the linear drive out to the center steering position and adjusted the heading of the compass, but once I turn it on, it just retracts and shuts off. So, I'm still looking for a bad connection somewhere. The truth of the matter with the electronic autopilot is that it will never work again on this voyage and is yet another victim of the cascading waterfall inside of Sailors Run. That unfortunate event allowed salt water to reach the circuitry inside the control module, and at the same time, it managed to take out the radar. I am feeling somewhat better, and it is a little warmer now that we are moving a few more degrees to the north. Last night, on the SSB radio, I could not hook up to Sailmail through Africa, as we are getting too far away from that area, but tonight, I was able to get an Australian station; although weak, it worked.

Today, I opened the sealed container on my last 3.5 dozen eggs to find that the storm managed to break eight of them. They were well-packed, but when one broke, the others began moving about.

DAY 102

I decided that, since losing the drogue in the last storm, in the next one, I will drag my "balls" off the back. Now, this might call for a little further explanation. You see, I have these two fiberglass fishing floats, about 20 inches in diameter in a woven line bag. I will shackle them to 35 feet of 3/8" chain hung on the end of the four hundred feet of line for the drogue, and I believe they should create a fair amount of drag. They are perhaps the only thing I could put out that would survive. These floats are a treasure Debbie and I salvaged in the Marshall Islands on the atoll of Mololap, in 2004. I have recently restrung the net bag that contains them with ¼ inch poly line, and they are ready to go.

Sailing the ocean blue, the Jefe'.

DAY 103

I'm feeling much better today, as obviously, the antibiotics have kicked in, and it seems that I have turned the corner on whatever was trying to pull me down.

We are sailing with double-reefed mizzen and Patches, the genoa. Wind and seas are gradually building, now blowing 30-40 knots with seas 15-18 feet. Patches had to be furled in and then I hoisted the staysail in its place. When I went forward to hoist the staysail, I was surprised to see the winch handle had been flipped overboard. This is the second locking handle I have lost on this voyage. I have never lost a handle in all the years of sailing until this trip, and the reason it's happening now is the new shallower boots that hold the handles. I recently replaced the old ones and should have realized right away that these were not going to be adequate. Now that leaves me with just two handles, and neither locks in place. This makes them dangerous to use, because when they pop out of the winches on the mast, they can very easily take your teeth out. Sometimes, you have to hang on to the handle just to stay in position by the mast, and that will never work with a handle that pops out. For now, I will not leave any more handles in the main-mast boot.

Later in the afternoon, I found myself hanging over the stern, replacing a pulley wheel at the bottom of the wind vane, as the old one was hanging up and chafing the lines.

DAY 104

Today, we are in the second day of the gale and charging along under staysail alone. Yesterday, when taking a shower, I noticed I have lost some weight, a difficult thing to notice with all the clothes I normally wear. I can't help but wonder why, as it seems I eat a lot. My explanation of the weight loss comes down to three theories:

1) Because I'm cold all the time, I find myself shivering at times, and that requires lots of calories to be spent.

2) The second logical thing is the "Whiskey Shakes", but without them, there would be days when I get no exercise at all.

3) My third, and possibly the biggest contributor to the weight loss, is being scared. You have heard of people being "scared straight." Well, I think just possibly you can be "Scared Skinny." Now just think of what a great new sailing term this is, like when you come in from a wild day of sailing on the bay, and someone asks, "How was the weather out there?" You can simply reply "Scared Skinny!"

DAY 105

Today is the third day in gale-force conditions, and since we are running under staysail alone, it requires very little sail handling. The one thing I did have to do was drop the staysail and reattach the hanks that were flipped out during a couple of hard pops the sail endured. It seems, once again, the problem occurred with the Lee Sail because the hanks have inferior springs, too weak to keep the hank closed when the sail pops. We are now pretty accustomed to dealing with such weather, but the only problem is the seas are up now, and it looks like something worse is heading our way and should arrive in about 36 hours, so "HANG ON!"

I realize I should have put an external antenna on the AIS unit. Down here at 45° south, the satellite coverage is not good, and occasionally, the AIS loses its position, setting off a very loud alarm. Last night, while I tried to sleep, the alarm was going off every minute, and I had to get up to cancel it. After about 15 alarms, I shut the F*en thing off. Then, an hour later, I turned it on only to have the same thing happen once again. I must assume I'm in a bad area and that things should improve as I close on Australia. I did find a way to cancel the alarm for no GPS position, and that is fine as it gets the position back within a minute anyhow.

"Scared Skinny", the Jefe'.

DAY 106

Today was water-the-batteries day, something I must do every two months. They are in the aft stateroom, our garage so-to-speak, with lots of things stored in there, not to mention all the black plastic bags full of plastic containers and wrappers that are piling up as the voyage continues. I also put in place the third storm board to eliminate the inboard waterfall. I had been reluctant to do this, as it makes opening the hatch much more difficult, not to mention climbing in and out. It's Valentine's Day, and I'm celebrating with an extra ration of chocolate bar and the beautiful card that Debbie had stashed aboard for this special time. She knows Valentine's Day has always been my favorite day, as it was the one holiday that I felt like I could afford!

DAY 107

Today is nice sailing, with winds down and "Patches" up. I pulled everything out of the back locker to gain access to the autopilot ram, so I could set it at the center steering position for more ohm readings and to get the model and serial # off the unit. Now I must wait to hear back from the manufacturer. This afternoon, the sun is out as we skirt along the southern inner edge of the high, hoping to stay out of the calm center. I'm getting great weather faxes out of Australia, so now there will be fewer surprises, weather-wise. There is a cold front that

The Jefe'

will hit early tomorrow and bring gale-force winds, forty knots or better.

DAY 108

Current Stats

Position
Lat. 46°08'S / Long. 115°55'E

Weather
Barometer = 1006 mb. -- Wind = 20-40 kts. - - Temp = 55°-63°

Seas
15-18 ft.

Distance
24 hr. run = 147 NM
Miles sailed last three days = 441 NM
Total miles sailed so far = 14,559 NM
Miles left to go to East Cape Tasmania = 1320 NM

Top speed so far
14.1 kts.

Today is a very special day as I sail along in yet another gale, and what makes it so special is we will, at last, have Cape Leeuwin abeam, our Third Cape of the Five.

Debbie and I would like to put a special shout out to all of our Aussie friends up there in Australia. We met many wonderful Aussies when we cruised there in 2004-2005 and have met many others in anchorages all over the world. You have a great country mates! It's amazing to think that I am sailing here in the waters of the folks from down under. The next and last two capes are not so far away now. There is East Cape Tasmania just 1400 NM and West Cape New Zealand just about 850 NM beyond that. These last two capes are very challenging as the weather in that area is notoriously difficult, and once again, you are down near the screaming 50° latitude in order to stay south of New Zealand. I will also be sailing close to land masses, and that always increases the "pucker factor." I must say a bit of good luck would go a long way towards easing the challenges that lay ahead for Sailors Run and crew. You can trust, I'm already watching the weather around those two capes.

DAY 109

Just wanted to mention Cape Leeuwin is the south-western most point of Australia, and it is named after the Dutch ship Leeuwin (Lioness) that charted much of the west coast in 1722. The ship is believed to be the first ship to visit there.

Many things seem to be happening today. First, the light in the galley mysteriously turns on by itself, and it is a new LED light. Upon closer examination, it is obvious that salt water is getting into the fixture and is creating a path for current to flow. While unscrewing the fixture, Sailors Run is slammed by a large wave, and I get tossed across the galley and slammed into the door frame, with my right shoulder blade and head taking most of the impact. My stocking hat goes flying, along with the battery light that I had strapped on my head. I see stars for a minute then regain my senses. After a few choice words, I realize, although nothing is broken, I still feel a serious pain in my shoulder and have a pretty good knot on the back of my head. Serious personal injury is very high on the "not-to-do list" for solo sailors.

Soon, it began raining hard, and I went topside to collect some much-needed water. I got about 10 gallons before the rain stopped. While crawling around on deck, I noticed a screw in the genoa track was pulled up, meaning the track was coming up while sailing with the genoa—not a good sign. As it turns out, the loose track was the source of the leak that was messing with the light in the galley, and this problem was actually created by me 11 years ago. In 2004, in Australia, I removed the teak decks on Sailors Run, and when I put the track back down where the genoa block goes, there were two bolts that went through the deck. The nuts on those bolts were under the piece of wood that the light in the galley was screwed to. Apparently, when I caulked those bolts in, I never pulled that light down to put on the washer and nuts. So, for the past 11 years, the lag screws in the deck carried the load but were now finally failing. Lucky for me, I found it before the track was broken.

Next, the coffee pot was launched off the stove by a wave and spilled water and coffee grounds all over the galley—this is the second time this trip that this has happened. Fortunately, the stove had not been lit yet, so the water was not hot, and I hadn't gotten the bungee cord on the pot. Now, when I finally get the coffee going, the second propane tank goes empty on me, so number three and my last propane tank is hooked up. I'm hoping this one can get me home. The winds have gone light, so I roll out Patches, only to discover another rip in the sail, so I immediately roll it back in. I would have pulled off the sail but feel my shoulder needs a day of rest before abusing it further. Later in the day, I hang over the stern tying new stopper knots on the servo rudder of wind vane, just a precaution so the old knots cannot fail.

DAY 110

Today, I cleaned the ground connections on the SSB radio for better performance and installed an additional heavy copper ground lead from the batteries to the engine as it seemed the engine was having trouble cranking over. The additional lead solved the problem, and the engine fired right up for its bi-weekly 15-minute oil circulating and dry out run in neutral.

DAY 111

Today, winds are 20-25 knots, and we are getting some warmer air, possibly off the great Australian desert. I like the warmer temperatures, but my eggs don't, as it seems every other one must be tossed. I don't eat them if they are cloudy or smell too bad; they can stink a little bit. Yet another cold front is closing in on us, and surely, things will get a little wilder soon. My variety of foods is dwindling, not to mention the cookies are all gone. I took a shower today, and that goes a long way in propping up one's spirits.

Doing the "Coffee Ground Shuffle" in the galley, the Jefe'.

DAY 112

Sailing along under mizzen, main and staysail in weather just a little too dicey to pull off "Patches" for repair. A cold front is sneaking up on us very slowly, making it difficult to judge when it will arrive. Tasmania looms ahead, surrounded by treacherous bodies of water, such as Bass Strait, Tasman Sea, and the Southern Ocean, where we will soon be. Here, I find myself with my back against the wall, as I have very little control over my arrival time. The area to the south of Tasmania is the spawning grounds of many severe low-pressure systems. Here aboard Sailors Run, I can only hope for a little good luck transiting this stretch of ocean.

DAY 113

Today, we are sailing fast along our course line, and it seems the high pressure in the area has stalled the cold front's arrival. There is a low-pressure trough up ahead, where we might have the opportunity to collect some water. I have decided that I will strip down to my underwear and slip on my Mustang work suit (a suit used by fisherman and Coast Guard when working in cold water areas). This is necessary because I'm getting down to my last warm clothing. Should I get a lot of water, then I can get some clothes washed.

Today, I wiped mold from some of the walls and oiled some of the teak wood below decks. It's funny how, before this voyage, I had a huge list of things to do to get the boat ready to go, and low and behold, once again, I have another large list of things that need to be done to the boat, a battle that seems impossible to win.

DAY 114

Today, I was pulling weather faxes and happened to notice a huge storm off Cape Horn, the likes of which no sailor would care to participate. It appeared two 964 lows had combined at the Horn and were tearing the place up. My weather has been reasonably mild the past 5 days, and it appears that will end tomorrow, when a big low moves up from the south onto Sailors Run. It appears I will be riding the northern top edge of the low in 35-45kt gale force conditions, and that should be OK. My only worry is if it comes in behind me and runs directly over the top of me, meaning much more severe conditions for a longer period of time. "Feeling Lucky Punk?"

Feeling lucky, the Jefe'.

DAY 115

It is "Barometer Soup" time as I watch the barometer plummet once again to 989 mb. A low has formed right in front of me, and I have sailed into the center of it. I go topside to harvest some much-needed water as it is raining like crazy, and I get about 35 gallons before the rain stops.

I now wait for the wind to fill in again, and when it does, I will probably have plenty. It takes about an hour, and the wind goes up to about 20 knots or less for the remainder of this day.

DAY 116

Today, I awoke to sunshine and a NW wind that is driving me to the south, so I jibe over and get back on course. I'm beginning to realize what it is like to live on a survival basis. It's almost like an experiment, where you isolate yourself from all sources of replenishment and interaction with other people. Mother Nature provides the challenges you must deal with daily, and good planning on the food supply will determine how well you will be nourished over the duration of the voyage. What fascinates me the most is the opportunity to study survival up close on a personal level. I know hunger is man's strongest driving force, with sex being the second strongest. I will cover "Sex of the single hander" in the next adventure.

What I have learned out here so far is that, with a year and a half to plan and obtain my needed supplies, I still fell short in some areas, and that was knowing I needed supplies for 5-7 months. What is truly frightening about this is thinking of how ill-prepared most families are for a prolonged isolation from food supplies. In the event of a catastrophe, whether it be a natural disaster, epidemic, war, a meteor hitting our planet, financial collapse etc., I believe most people would be in trouble in three days and forced to go ask for provisions. It would not be long after that, they would go steal the stuff at whatever risk. This is just food for thought from an isolated sailor, with way too much time on his hands!

DAY 117

Current Stats

Position
Lat. 46°23'S / Long. 142°25'E

Weather
Barometer = 986 mb. -- Wind = 45-60 kts. - - Temp = 55°-58°

Seas
15-30 ft.

Distance
24 hr. run = 142 NM
Miles sailed last three days = 389 NM
Total miles sailed so far = 15,783 NM
Miles left to go to East Cape Tasmania = 210 NM

Top speed so far
14.1 kts.

Today, the winds are blowing 45 knots plus, and the seas are getting up to the twenty-foot range. I'm sailing under staysail alone and exceeding 7 knots at times. The low continues to strengthen as it moves to the SE towards New Zealand. At

The Jefe'

1:30p.m., I'm forced to go to bare poles, as the winds are gusting 60+ knots, and by 7p.m., after recording 12.1 knots on the odometer, it's time to set out the drogue once again. I use the fishing floats in the net bag with a swivel, about 30 feet of 3/8" chain, and 400 feet of 5/8 three strand and never exceed 5 knots after that.

At 3:30a.m., I drag the drogue back in, as the fierce squalls have abated, and stay under bare poles for another 5 hours in 45 knots. We spent 18 hours under bare poles; eight of that was with the drogue deployed and the drogue dug in and did a great job. The difference with this storm from the last, is that it was of shorter duration, and the sustained winds were a little less. Although it did not produce the enormous seas, we were slammed many times by breaking waves, and it was extremely dangerous sailing.

I believe during this storm I witnessed my first "white squall." I first noticed it when I came up on deck with winds sustained at around 50 knots and not a cloud in the sky anywhere, except what appeared to be a very low white cloud stretching across the surface of the ocean. While I observed this phenomenon, I suddenly realized what I was seeing, and it was not a cloud at all but rather sea spray being ripped from the surface of the waves that were now running at over 30 feet. I quickly dove below, battening down the companionway before the squall hit. The winds must have exceeded 70 knots and just pummeled the boat with salt spray. By the time I got my camera ready to go and went back topside, it was over. This was definitely a phenomenon of nature like I have never seen before. I shiver at the thought of the disaster that could have happened if caught off-guard with sails up when something like that occurred.

Hanging on once again, the Jefe'.

DAY 118

First, let me say I shared some of this day in the last adventure because I could and wanted you to know I was all right. The winds screeched and howled throughout the night, and on many occasions, Sailors Run was slammed by powerful breaking waves, but little water found its way below. I rolled out of my berth at 3 am after riding on the drogue for 8 hours and decided to winch it in. Now, I have to tell you, this thing really bites into the sea and takes nearly an hour to get it back onboard. I decide to remain under bare poles until the squalls subside a bit. Our run for this day was diminished because of the time under the drogue. It was very late in the day that the winds began to come down, and the waves diminished at a much slower rate. The only damage we sustained was the loss of a dozen eggs that were broken in the fridge, leaving me three eggs. As it turned out, these were also rotten, so possibly, they were all finished before the storm struck anyway!

DAY 119

It appears today we will get a break from the severe weather with more severe weather returning tomorrow. I find myself sailing along the bottom of Tasmania about 100+ miles to the south headed for the East Cape, Tasmania. It appears the Cape will not be reached on this day. Late in the day, the winds increase to 45 knots. I sail on under staysail alone and have very rough seas overnight.

DAY 120

After 119 days 4 hours and 11 minutes, Sailors Run sails abeam of South East Cape Tasmania! "Yahoo" our fourth cape and now off to cape #5, New Zealand, about 850 NM to the east south east. Tasmania is an Island State of Australia, where over 1/2 million people live. The Island, nearly 100 miles square, was first sited by the Dutch sailing captain Abel Tasman in 1642. He named the Island Van Diemen's land after the prime minister of the Dutch East Indies for whom he sailed. Tasman is believed to be the first European to site Australia, and it is also believed the Aborigines had lived there for more than 40,000 years prior to that sighting.

I'm currently watching the barometer shoot up like it has a solid fuel booster rocket attached to it. This means we are approaching the high pressure that will eventually bring us northerly winds to take us south southeast down around the high to get to New Zealand. The 975 low that has been tormenting us over the past three days should move south east and away, taking the bad weather with it.

I know there was another topic I was to explore, but for some reason, possibly battle fatigue, I can't recall what it was. Hmmm! 40,000 years ago, maybe we did all fall down from the "Milky Way".

Closing on that final Cape, the Jefe'.

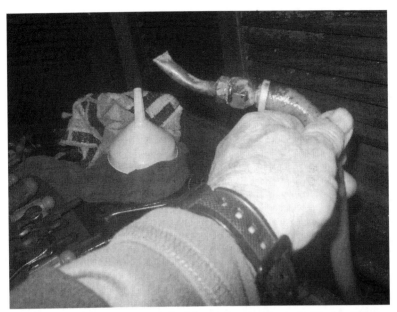

Propane feed line that failed from extreme gimbaling action.

On top of a large wave, not much of this wild ocean looks good.

Sailors Run being pushed ahead under bare poles in large seas.

Chapter 10: Days 121-140

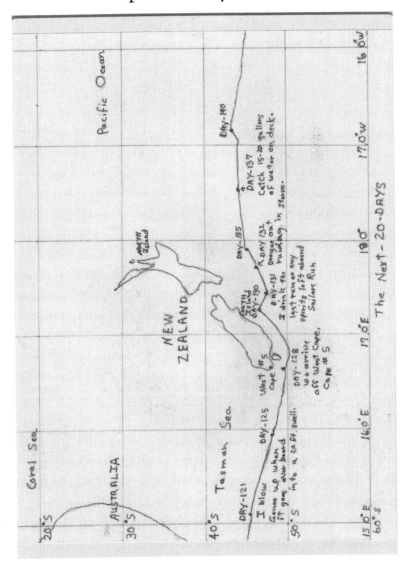

Coral Sea

AUSTRALIA

Pacific Ocean

NEW ZEALAND

NORTH Zealand

Tasman Sea

DAY-121
I blow up when 7ft gag over board. Game up into a 20 ft swell.

DAY-125 West Cape #5

SOUTH Zealand DAY-190

DAY-128 Ws arrive off West Cape, Cape #5

#DAY-131 I admit the last run or any spirits left aboard. Sailors Ruin

#DAY-132 Drogue out Pui & bag in storm.

DAY-135

DAY-137 Catch 15-20 gallons of water on deck.

DAY-140

The Next-20-DAYS

20°S
30°S
40°S
50°S
60°S
15.0°E
140°E
17.0°E
180°
170°W
160°W

DAY 121

Have you ever had one of those days when you wished you had just stayed in bed? For me, it was day #121. This day was dominated by light winds out of the south east, the direction we needed to go. I consider myself a pretty good sailor, but on several occasions in my life, I have found myself not being able to get there from where I was under sail. This night, the air was light on the nose with a 15ft southerly swell and some current against us. I have no genoa to put up yet, and the main boom is broken. With the wind vane, I need about 7 knots of wind for it to perform and we have 5. The only two directions it seems I can go is either northeast or northwest, and I want to go south east.

The wind will eventually fill in from the north, but in the meantime, I'm going the wrong way. I took the helm, and if I was really careful, I could go SW-SSW, which was better than nothing, but it was now dark, and I needed to sleep. It seems, after about an hour of experimenting with different sail trim and adjustments on the Monitor wind vane, at last, I was able to get the boat sailing itself to the SW. Knowing the wind was going to fill in from the North, at last, I could get some sleep.

It finally got light, and I decided I would pull down "Patches" [the genoa] for repairs. I grab a quick, cold cereal breakfast and then set about gathering what I needed to patch the sail. Once up on deck, I noticed the sheet line to the staysail was failing, as it was down to the center core. Now, I must pull everything out of the aft compartment, the 60lb. CQR anchor, 1000 feet of line, as well as a heap of other miscellaneous gear to get the much-needed replacement sheet line. I replace it and reverse the other one, as it seems, in the past storms, it chafes on the forward lower shroud of the main mast. While I'm getting the caulking gun loaded with silicone, I suddenly here this "loud pop" and there goes the main, as the main sheet has now parted and the 4-inch block that is attached to

140

the clew is flying wildly. This is an easy fix, as I have plenty of main sheet and have only lost about 7ft of it where the break occurred. At last, I roll out "Patches", pull her out of the foil, and get her down on the deck. I'm pleasantly surprised to see she only has the one tear in the sail, unlike usual, where I find 2-5 more once it's down.

Soon, the patch is back on, and I begin to feed the sail into the furler foil. This is not easy single-handed, and after about 6 trips to the foil and back to the mast, I have the sail about halfway up. I pull more slack and line up the luff cord, so it will enter the foil once again, then go back to the mast and start to crank it up. Suddenly, a gust of wind of about 15 knots hits us and blows the sail off the deck and over the side. At first, I'm not too concerned, as I believe there isn't enough sail to reach the water, but much to my surprise, we roll hard to starboard as a 15-foot swell is coming through, and Patches scoops up tons of water and disintegrates right before my eyes. I mean, she tears all along the foot just above the UV cover of the sail and up the leach of the sail; she blows a seam in the middle of the sail, and another section rips from foot to Leach. I drag the pieces aboard and look at the tatters and the bottom paint that is now all over it, and for an instant, I can visualize myself throwing the whole "damn thing" over the side.

In my mind, I have had enough of this piece of "shit sail" and all that it has put me through so far. So, why not just be rid of it and never have to worry about sewing on this "son-of-a-bitch" again? No! I can't throw away the sail as I need it in some lighter winds that will surely occur along the route back to Ecuador. So, what if I now have about 60 feet of repair work to do on the sail? This might take a week or more, but I can do it, so why not?

DAY 122

Today, Sailors Run is sailing along nicely on course for West Cape New Zealand. I spent over 8 hours sewing on Patches, making some progress. Today was also the warmest day I have seen in the Southern Ocean, 67°.

I have a very interesting study going on with various types of mold found aboard and have come to realize there are some major differences. Now, take the green mold that grows on the cheese and 4-month old bread; this mold has kind of a sharp bite to it, like extra sharp cheddar cheese. But let me tell you, it is nothing compared to the black mold that was lurking in the bottom of my oatmeal box. I took a bite of my charcoal colored oatmeal, and "Holy Damn" that was a *wild-assed* taste. I was spitting out that stuff and could not get that taste out of my mouth and throat.

It was after about 15 minutes that my lips started feeling numb, and my face started to tingle. My hands even felt tingly. I was starting to get worried. I had already chucked the oatmeal overboard and had eaten a bowl of cold cereal, thinking that would absorb whatever little bit of it that went down my throat, but it seemed to be getting worse. I finally made myself a cup of lime juice, put a couple of shots of rum in it, and guzzled that down, and remarkably, that seemed to make me feel much better. I don't know what to say except to hell with that "waste not want not" program I had going on!

DAY 123

Sailing along nicely today and spent another 10 hours working on "Patches". We did get some rain from the remnants of the cyclone Winston that had hit Fiji as a category-5 and then drifted our way. Other than that, I feel mostly just tired.

Just hanging in there, the Jefe'.

DAY 124

It was about midnight on a restless night aboard Sailors Run. I was having trouble sleeping, as the air had become light, and the sails were banging about topside, caused by being continually tossed about in the confused seas. Finally, I had enough and rolled out of my bunk, dragging the spinnaker out from under the chart table, wrestling it up the companionway stairs and out over the top of the three storm boards into the cockpit. Now that will get your heart pumping.

This spinnaker is a very large one that came from a Gulf Star 50 that my son owned. He gave it to me, knowing I needed one, and it was brand new. Debbie and I had it cut down in Argentina to fit the Sailors Run. The sail is amazingly powerful with very broad shoulders and will move Sailors Run at 5-6 knots in 10 knots of breeze. I launched the spinnaker, and soon, we are moving at near 3 knots, and with a little help from the mizzen trim, the wind vane is barely able to steer.

I finally crash out below and dream the spinnaker wrapped itself tightly around the forestay, and I was aloft in the boson's chair frantically slashing away at it with a butcher knife, trying to cut it clear before the next gale strikes.

We sailed under spinnaker for 9 hours before the winds increased to 15 knots, and it was time to snuff it, no easy feat for sure. Once on the foredeck, I "clipped in" after having already released the spinnaker sheet line and started the tug of war to bring the sock down over the wildly popping and snapping spinnaker. Only by standing up on the foredeck, taking three wraps around my hand, and falling back using all my weight, ending up lying on the deck, at last, I get this "monster" contained in the snuffer. I must admit, it is times like this that you wonder if flying a spinnaker is really a good idea for the solo sailor.

DAY 125

Today was a light air day, once again, and I was becalmed [no wind] for 8 hours. At last, we start moving along with a favorable breeze that filled in from the north.

At times like this I get a little nervous lingering in an area of notoriously bad weather and having to struggle to get my "ass" out of here. If I was not sailing unassisted around the world, I would have that motor on and scooting out of here, but that is not what this voyage is about.

Today, I sewed on "Patches" for 7 hours. Then I got my weekly shower, something that really makes me feel so much better. I have eaten the last of the potatoes, although I do have some instant mashed potatoes, and tonight, it will be a can of "Chunky Clam Chowder" and a can of corn for dinner.

DAY 126

Current Stats

Position
Lat. 47°10'S / Long. 162°22'E

Weather
Barometer = 1007 mb. -- Wind = 8-25 kts. - - Temp = 57°-62°

Seas
6-10 ft.

Distance
24 hr. run = 125 NM
Miles sailed last three days = 267 NM
Total miles sailed so far = 16,744 NM
Miles left to go to West Cape New Zealand = 150 NM

Top speed so far
14.1 kts.

So far, the weather looks great for getting around West Cape New Zealand, although possibly a little light at times. I put in yet another 8 hours sewing on "Patches", and there is still no end in sight to this project. All of this handwork truly "sucks and blows." Wait a minute, possibly I have just defined the "sex life of the single hander"! Now, getting back to the sewing, I think the fingers on my left hand have more needle holes in them than a "bear's paw stealing honey from a bee's nest."

Now practicing the 3-SSS's-Sun, Sailing and Sewing, the Jefe'.

DAY 127

Today, we are closing on New Zealand. It is called the land of the great white cloud, and lo and behold, I saw the cloud, but New Zealand remained invisible.

I got on the SSB this a.m. at 1900 U.T.C. and talked to Ed on the sailing vessel. AKA Ed is the net controller filling in for Jim Bandy, who is in Fiji. This will continue until Jim gets his new radio and generator going after cyclone "Winston" took them out. Ed was the first human being I had spoken to in 127 days, and that was really strange, as it seems your voice is something you have to use, or it goes away. I had a hard time being able to carry on a very long conversation. The radio frequency down here is 8173.0 USB.

Debbie and I would like to put a shout out to our many great New Zealand friends, as well as our Kiwi friends from all over the world.

DAY 128

Today is a monumental day of the adventure, as Sailors Run pulls abeam of West Cape New Zealand after 127 days 11 hours and 55 minutes. This is our 5th and final cape, and now, I must say, "Debbie I'm coming home"—keep a light on. As we came in under the Cape, we were about 8 miles north of the Snare Islands, and I could actually see them. The first land I have seen since Cape Horn, and I must admit, although not so large, they were green and looked pretty inviting for this sailor.

It is a rainy day here, south of New Zealand, and I want to thank all of you out there for your prayers and best wishes as I have arrived here in pretty good shape. The Barometer soup is about to kick in, and the next 5 days look like they will be rough, easing on Friday.

Tonight, as darkness fell, a front arrived out of the SE, and I had 40-50 knots of wind. Under staysail alone, I recorded a speed in excess of 13 knots. The good thing is I can get into open ocean and fight it out with what's coming next. One of the worst things is, it's going to blow like Hell from the NW then switch around to the SW, where a big swell is being created. A low that is coming up over New Zealand and pushing up against the high is creating a squash zone that will intensify the winds in the area. I suspect there will be 45-50 knots with extremely rough seas, and this will be at its worst on Thursday. I'm currently shooting north in 35 knots of wind under staysail alone, trying to avoid the worst of the low that is coming. Only time will tell how this all works out.

DAY 129

Today, it is a windy and sunny day as we reach to the north. The winds are starting to die down as this day progresses, but that will be short-lived as that Northwester should fill in by morning. Early this a.m., I had a wave break on Sailors Run, and a small amount of water came through any breach it could find or create. I now have over 50 hours of handwork into repairing "Patches" and still much more to go.

I just love the thoughtfulness of many of you out there. I even had one caring person offer to bring me food if I needed it since I was so close to New Zealand. I truly appreciate the thought, but as you know, the rules say "Unassisted," which means no such help. But it sure felt great to know how much people are willing to do to keep Sailors Run and crew going.

Getting "Battle Ready" for what's coming!

DAY 130

Great sailing day with lots of sunshine, as we try to get north, hoping to avoid the worst of a low that is headed our way. I spend the day pumping bilges, applying chafe protection where needed, and looking for anything that might need attention before the winds hit. Oh yes, and of course sewing on "Patches." The local VHF Radio has been putting out storm warnings every two hours all day, with predictions of 60 knots on both ends of New Zealand. I'm very happy to be away from the south end at this time.

Darkness comes, and I feel a certain sense of anxiety, possibly because we have had to deal with so much severe weather during this voyage that I wonder if our luck can keep holding out. This one looks to be bad because there is going to be a 4-meter swell from the NW, and the main punch will be a SW swell of five meters. That spells amazingly rough seas ahead, "washing machine" seas.

DAY 131

Still waiting, yet still not much going on, and I start to question the weather forecast. More sewing on "Patches."

We are running up against shortages on Sailors Run, and today, a significant one occurred. I spliced the "main brace" for the final time, as the rum stores are now completely depleted. This is an amazing happenstance as I had an efficiency expert, my friend John, who owns restaurants in Colorado, sit down with me and explain my alcohol ration for this voyage. I gave John my total inventory of rum, tequila, and other various spirits, and he had computed all of this based on me returning within 6 months. John told me, "Jefe'", you can have three drinks a day, but you cannot have four." I assured John that was perfect, yet he reminded me once again, "You cannot have four." Well, you have probably figured out by now that, with still nearly 50 days left to go to reach the 6-month supply limit, a major shortfall has occurred. There can only be two explanations; either John can't add worth a shit, or these storms have been far more devastating on the crew of Sailors Run than humanly possible.

Does anyone out there have a set of plans for a still?

DAY 132

I was just two hours into the day when the storm force winds hit Sailors Run, and of course, it was night-time! We were sailing along comfortably with mizzen and staysail when 50 knots of wind pounced upon us. I scrambled out of my berth and suited up as fast as possible.

Once out on deck, the fury of the screeching winds and driving rain quickly set the tone for things to come. I pulled down the wildly flapping mizzen sail, and in the process, somehow, the mizzen boom popped free of its gooseneck and flailed around precariously, wanting to do damage to someone or something. Fortunately, I had a mast step folded out, and the boom came to rest on that, and by tightening the mizzen sheet, the boom stayed secured, pinned to the step. The sail also found its way down out of the mast and was thrashing about. At long last, I was able to wrap the sail around and around the boom and lash it down.

I crept forward, staying clipped in and praying not to be engulfed by huge breaking seas while attempting to drop the staysail before it self-destructed. The staysail came down with little trouble and was soon lashed down on deck.

We sailed on under bare poles, driven to the north for the next seven hours. It was then, with rapidly growing waves, I decided to put out the drogue. While deploying the drogue, a large breaking wave filled the cockpit and drenched me to the bone, once again, not so much different from the driving rain when I was taking the sails down.

Now, I have a bit of a problem, as I have no dry warm clothing, except a scarf to wrap around my neck, a jacket that I call my sleeping jacket that never goes topside, and two dry stocking hats. Because some of my gear is wool, it will keep me warm even though damp, and by sleeping in this gear all wrapped up in blankets with my hot Tequila bottle, my clothes will eventually get nearly dry.

After 11 hours under bare poles, the winds begin to drop, and I haul in the drogue that has been out for the past 4 hours.

Days 121-140

Once again, the staysail and mizzen are back up in 25-30 knots, and we are headed for the International Date Line. I'm still out here and still going, the Jefe'.

DAY 133

Today, there is very little going on, as we are becalmed for 12 hours, and the wind is very light when it finally returns. The high has come upon us and centered over top of us. I just can't seem to win; when I go north to get away from the storms, I get becalmed then force myself to sail more to the south in search of stronger winds. We are still unable to reach the Date Line at 180° Longitude, and of course, I sewed on "Patches" for another eight hours.

DAY 134

Today is sunny and pretty good weather for drying out clothes, but the winds are too light to allow the wind vane to steer. I spend most of my day running up and down from sewing to getting the boat back on course, something I did at least 30 times with little results; however, "Patches" got 8 hours of my time once again.

DAY 135

Today, Sailors Run passed another milestone, crossing Longitude 180° and back into the Western Hemisphere. "Yahooooo!" This happened after 134 days and 14 hours at sea. Now, I will be counting down the longitude to 85°, where at a distance of 400NM off the coast of Chile, we make the turn north for Bahía Caraquez, Ecuador.

Today, "Patches" got yet another 8 hours of my time, and I'm happy to report that I'm working on the last tear, which is about 18.5 feet Long. This tear requires 7-rows of zig-zag stitches by hand. It seems I have little time for much else now and cannot respond to very many emails. I did get a much-needed shower today, once again, brightening my spirits.

The Jefe'
Making it right with "Patches", the Jefe'.

DAY 136

Today was good sailing in sunshine, although rain is expected overnight, so possibly, I can collect some much-needed water.

Yesterday, while replacing the failed hose clamp on the wind vane that was holding the two washer halves in place, ensuring a good mesh of the gears, I noticed many gooseneck barnacles attached to the stern. I decided it was time to try to scrape the bottom of the boat that was reachable by hanging over the side. I went to get the boat hook that I had planned to attach my scraper to and decided to look over the side to see what kind of a job was ahead of me. I could not believe it! There were absolutely no barnacles on the sides, and the bottom paint appeared clean. Yahoo! So I left the barnacles on the stern for now as I have too much to do already with "Patches" getting so much of my time.

While on deck, I noticed a pod of approximately 30 dolphins circling a school of fish and going after them. The dolphins were perhaps the largest, fattest ones I have ever seen, looking almost like small killer whales.

DAY 137

The winds were light overnight then picked up to 25 knots about daylight, and Sailors Run was happily bounding across the Pacific once again. I sewed for 7 hours on "Patches" and was able to complete 18 inches of the 18 ft. 6-inch tear. I think I'm getting faster. It started a steady rain in the morning. I got up on deck and was able to collect 15-20 gallons of water.

I have been "Jefe'" the chef'. Three days ago, I made some chicken spaghetti and was amazed how much noodles I ended up with. Having a good lot of it for dinner, I still had enough for another 3 days. I put the leftovers in the refrigerator that doesn't work, and that made me feel better about saving it. Tonight was the fourth night of the well-fermented spaghetti, and I noticed it was mostly noodles, so I added a can of mixed vegetables and a can of tuna, and voilà, we were back in business. I know I must be making you very hungry, and I'm so, so sorry.

Today, we passed 40 NM south of the Chatham Islands, a group of Islands claimed by New Zealand. Only two out of the 12 islands are inhabited due to the windy rainy weather, and the population is only about 200 people.

DAY 138

Current Stats

Position
Lat. 44°22'S / Long. 172°15'W

Weather
Barometer = 1015 mb. -- Wind = 10-15 kts. - - Temp = 58°-62°

Seas
6-8 ft.

Distance
24 hr. run = 117 NM
Miles sailed last three days = 321 NM
Total miles sailed so far = 18,028 NM
Miles left to go to turn North = 3518 NM

Top speed so far
14.1 kts.

Last night, I chatted with a Kiwi fisherman by the name of Rex on the "Thomas Harrison," a very large commercial fishing boat. We were passing like two ships in the night within 6 NM of each other, and he gave me a call on the VHF radio. He explained it had been a long time since he had seen any boats out here and was curious about where I might be headed. As you can imagine, he got very interested in the voyage as I shared with him about what I was doing. I asked him how the fishing was, and he said it was great, as the New Zealand fishery does a fine job of managing the resource. He also said to keep a look out for a very large sperm whale that hangs out in the waters we were passing through. He had seen him many times over the last thirty years of fishing, and he said the sperm whale is after the same kind of fish he is fishing for. It was some time later after getting off the radio that I wondered, how does the giant sperm whale catch the fish, by sneaking up on them?

Out sailing and making new acquaintances in the remote Southern Ocean, the Jefe'.

DAY 139

Today is nice sailing in moderate winds. I still have no sighting of the sperm whale. The sperm whale is different from most whales, as it is not a filter feeder but is carnivorous and eats fish. It has also been known to attack sailboats and sink them after they rammed into it by accident as the whale slept on the surface at night, and I guess that's fair enough. I have never seen one and certainly would like to, especially if it was in my path, hopefully before I hit it.

I have some concerns with the Monitor Wind Vane since it is the only thing between me and my having to hand-steer the rest of the way back. There seems to be excessive play in the shaft from which the servo rudder is suspended and swings back and forth on. Right now, I'm just lubricating it regularly, hoping to reduce the wear. Of course, I spent another 7 hours sewing on "Patches." Oh well, it makes the days fly by quickly.

DAY 140

Today, I'm plagued by light SE winds that are forcing me more to the north, and I need to get south to the 46° to stay in the wind.

After my normal 7 hours of sewing on Patches, I glued on 6 small patches with Hypalon Glue that I would normally use for patching the inflatable dinghy. The glue seemed to work great, and I believe I will avoid future tears that would have come from these small holes that were developing.

Days 121-140

I'm happy to report that I had my last green bread tuna sandwich today and discarded the remaining half loaf of 20-week old bread. Please don't try this with organic bread, as I'm sure you would need a jack hammer to tenderize it before eating after two weeks. I'm a little concerned that my cholesterol level is possibly getting too low, as I have no red meat, chips, eggs, or any of the other good stuff left to eat. I'm thinking that I can possibly warm up a half a cup of lard each day and drink it with a little sugar and cinnamon. It might be like eating pie crust without the crust. "I just don't know what to think about this." Oh well, don't worry. I might just be feeling the side effects of the last "green tuna sandwich".

New Dodger keeping the water out, while pounding to weather.

Monster wave moves in on us during storm east of New Zealand.

Riding tethered to drogue during storm east of New Zealand.

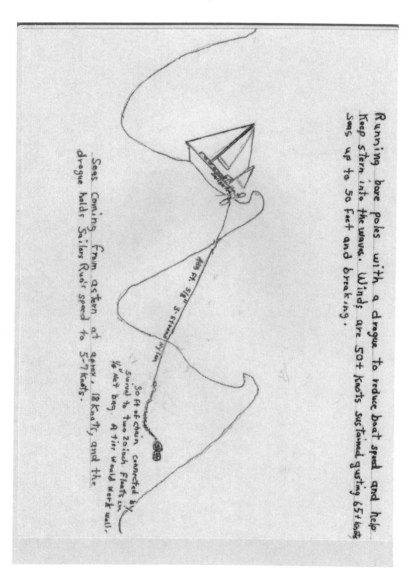

Running bare poles with a drogue to reduce boat speed and help keep stern into the waves. Winds are 50+ knots sustained gusting 65+ knots. Seas up to 50 feet and breaking.

50 ft. 3-strand nylon

30 ft of chain connected by swivel to two 20-inch floats in ½" net bag. A tire would work well.

Seas coming from astern at approx. 18 knots, and the drogue holds Sailors Run's speed to 5-7 knots.

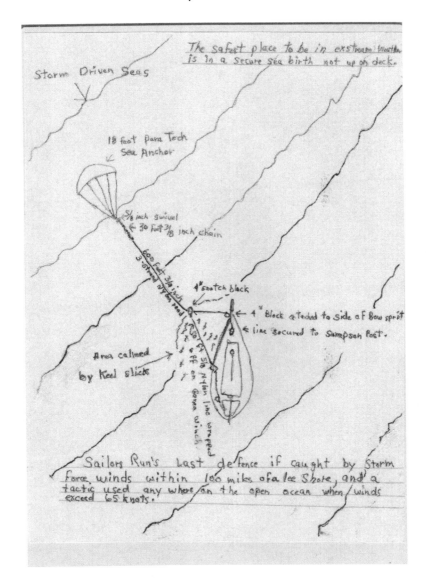

The safest place to be in extreme weather is in a secure sea birth not up on deck.

Storm Driven Seas

18 foot Para Tech Sea Anchor

5/8 inch swivel

30 feet 3/8 inch chain

300 feet 3/8 inch 3-strand nylon road

4" snatch block

4" block attached to side of Bow sprit

line secured to Sampson Post.

Area calmed by Keel slick

5/8 nylon line wrapped to Genoa winch

Sailors Run's Last defence if caught by Storm force winds within 100 miles of a lee Shore, and a tactic used any where on the open ocean when winds exceed 65 knots.

Chapter 11: Days 141-160

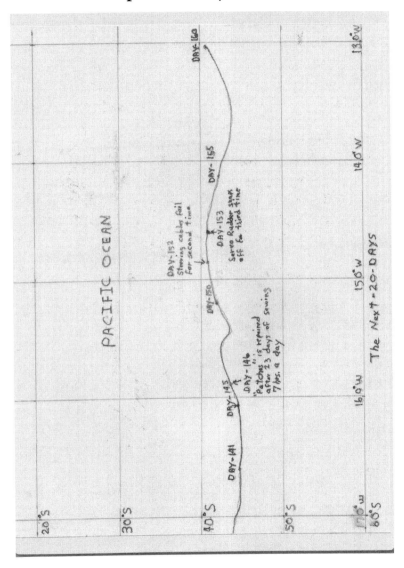

PACIFIC OCEAN

DAY-141

DAY-145

DAY-146
"Patches" is repaired
after 23 days of sewing
7 hrs. a day

DAY-150

DAY-152
Showing cables fail
for second time

DAY-153
Servo Rudder stock
off for third time

DAY-155

DAY-160

The Next 20 DAYS

20°S

30°S

40°S

50°S

60°S

170°W

160°W

150°W

140°W

130°W

DAY 141

Spent most of this day becalmed in glassy seas, all the time working on "Patches".

You may have heard that a recent "Kon Tiki 2" expedition from Peru to Easter Island with two balsa wood rafts that had planned to sail back to Chile was cut short. They say this was due to the El Nino weather pattern that was forcing them too far to the south. A total of 12-people were rescued by a ship that was diverted to their location after a Chilean military plane had located them. What concerns me is these two rafts could very well end up on my return route, as they are drifting north in the Humboldt Current. I believe they left locator beacons on the rafts, so I will possibly have their positions and can avoid them. If they left any rum onboard, I would surely go find them. Does anyone have their list of provisions?

Practicing my light-to-no-air sailing skills, the Jefe'.

DAY 142

Today, sailing in very light winds, once again, as the high pressure begins to move over us. Of course, I sewed on "Patches" for 7 hours and believe the end of this project is just a couple of days away. I don't know if Sailors Run will set any records, but I'm pretty sure we will have the record for the most patches ever put on a genoa underway by hand.

DAY 143

Today, sailing is a little faster in light air, and of course, "Patches" gets her 7 hours.

I will mention at this time; there were two other boats that I know of that were attempting solo circumnavigations via the 5 Great Capes this year, and neither attempt has been successful. The first I heard about was a very brave lady, Donna Lang, sailing on a 28-foot Southern Cross sailboat. She made it around four of the capes, but on her approach to Cape Horn, she was knocked down twice in one hour, sustaining damage to some of her equipment. In view of the horrific weather taking place at Cape Horn, she made a prudent judgment call. She then sailed north up the west coast of South America to finish her circumnavigation via the Panama Canal and back to the east coast from where she started.

The second vessel I heard about was a Fast-40 sailed by Joe Harris, who was attempting to break the 137-day world record. He had to put in twice for repairs, and the last time he had delamination on three to four feet of the bow of his boat, so he threw in the towel. So now, just know the Jefe' and his war horse, Sailors Run, are praying we make it to the finish line. Debbie and I are very familiar with the Fast-40, as it was the boat that beat us in the 2010 Fernando De Noronha Regatta, the largest sailboat race in Brazil. He never got properly measured to compete in his own division, so they dropped him into our cruising boat division, and we had to race him straight up with no handicap. We had two good friends from Argentina as crew, Hector and Patricia, and after 300nm, the Fast-40 beat us to the finish line by only 40 minutes. We ended up coming in second.

DAY 144

Today is a most welcome day for me, as "Patches" is once again back in one piece and ready to fly. After 23 days and over 140 hours of hand sewing, my war horse has her most powerful working sail ready to go back on the furler when the wind conditions will allow it!

Once I had "Patches" folded up and ready to go on deck, I pulled out the bathroom scale and jumped on it to see what was left of the Jefe'. Well, I weighed 155lbs when I started this adventure, and I'm now weighing in at a lean, mean 138lbs. This is less than I weighed in the 5th-grade or when training for marathons; at those times, my weight was at least 139 lbs. I might be on to something here and am thinking about starting Jefe''s offshore weight loss clinics, where you sail offshore for

30 days and only take enough provisions for 15. Results will be guaranteed, but I know I don't want to be the one guarding the ship's stores! These cruises could also be good for alcoholics, as when I ran out of Rum, I never even missed it. I think it had a lot to do with the fact that there is just no availability that would cause one to think about being tempted to have something to drink. Wow, we are learning so much cool stuff on this voyage!

Tonight, I made gravy with Kirkland canned chicken in it and poured that over a pile of instant mashed potatoes with a can of vegetables and voilà! A great dinner was had. I actually had leftovers for two more nights, so I put them in the Refrigerator-That-Doesn't-Work.

DAY 145

Slow today, sailing as close to the wind as we can go and pounding into the waves. I decided the weather was finally right to put "Patches" back up, so I wrestled the 50 lb. sail up the companionway steps and attempted to bench press it through the narrow opening. After what seemed like way too long a struggle, I ended up balancing the sail on my head while trying to clear the edges where it was hanging up. I made that final all you can do bench-press, and I mean it was like trying to bench-press a Buick. It felt as if I was trying to lift the cabin top off the boat.

Out of go-hetas (push in Spanish), I let the sail fall back into the galley and regrouped. I try again and put the sail in a sail bag then crank it up with the mizzen halyard. It was out in the cockpit in no time. It is then that the wind begins to pick up, and I had to stuff "Patches" back down through the hatch from where she had just emerged. You see, I'm not going to try to hoist this thing in a blow, where it could once again go in the ocean.

I spent the rest of the morning wiping down the surfaces of the galley with vinegar to get rid of the mold that is taking up residence in my all-too-moist environment.

DAY 146

We sailed a good course through the night, and the winds were now down. It was time to put up "Patches" before breakfast. Once again, it was a wrestling match getting the sail out of the boat, out around the mizzen rigging, and finally up onto the foredeck. I carefully began raising the sail, checking countless times to be sure it was going in the foil correctly, and staying aboard at the same time. At last, "Patches" was up and flying. After making fast the halyard, I stepped around the staysail to admire my repair job. I almost felt ill, as I found myself looking at yet another 4-inch tear in "Patches". The sail had to come back down. Back down on deck, the repair was easy, and this time, I used a product called Grab It, a Loctite product for gluing down flooring, as at this point, I'm running out of everything.

Once again, I start hauling the sail back up into the foil. It was about ¾ of the way up when the sail jammed in the foil. The sail was in ahead of the 5mm luff line, and I mean, it was jammed. I worked on it for over two hours and was still unable to pull it free. Finally, in desperation, I got my Exacto Razor Knife and was ready to try to cut it in the clear, not a real good thing. I decided at the last minute to make one more attempt to get the feed alignment piece off the foil; on earlier attempts, one of the screws would just not budge. I had been spraying WD-40 on everything, hoping something would loosen up, and at last, I got the feed unit off, pounding it down the sail and free. Then, with my vise grips, I was able to tug the sail free of the foil it was jammed into.

After 7.5 hours, "Patches" was up and flying, and I could go drown my "cotton mouth" in coffee and some much-needed breakfast. I counted the patches on "Patches," and she

The Jefe'

now has 43. That is not counting the big, major ones of the last repair job.

DAY 147

Current Stats
Position
Lat. 45°13'S / Long. 157°00'W
Weather
Barometer = 1013 mb. -- Wind = 5-8 kts. - - Temp = 60°-63°
Seas
2-4 ft.
Distance
24 hr. run = 38 NM
Miles sailed last three days = 300 NM
Total miles sailed so far = 18,877 NM
Miles left to go to turn North = 2972 NM
Top speed so far
14.1 kts.

Today, I am slowly moving along 45° of latitude in very light air. Normally, the highs would be above me and the lows to the south, but it seems some highs are south of me, creating head winds on the nose at times. Having "Patches" up when there is no wind is like having a powerful motor with dual 4-barrel carburetors and no gas. Oh well, this is all part of sailing, never quite knowing what you will get from day to day.

Limping along the 45° South Latitude in the not so "Roaring 40s", The Jefe'.

DAY 148

I awoke this a.m. to Sailors Run moving along smoothly and pretty much on course. By the time I got up, we had altered course and seemed to be going due north. I go out on deck to ascertain what is happening and realize we are surrounded by many micro wind systems, and to make it even worse, "Patches" has yet another 4-inch tear in her. I feel like going below and looking in the mirror and asking myself, "Is this really happening?" I decide, screw it, I'm going to have breakfast before tackling "Patches". After coffee and breakfast, Patches is down on deck. I put on patch #44, and the sail goes back up quite smoothly.

Once again, we are sailing along at speed. I decide to tack over, as this course is almost due north; after the tack, Sailors Run settles in on due south. This is very disappointing, tacking through 180°. It is obvious, with the seas on the nose and adverse current, I have virtually stopped all forward progress to the east. I tack back to the north to get over the low that is to the NE of me. Once the sails are trimmed in, I notice Patches now has an 18-inch tear in the middle of it. Holy Shit, what next? I refuse to bring down the sail again. The wind is rising, so I roll it in so only 1/3rd is exposed and the tear is buried. I know this is hard on the sail, but at this point, I just want to get some use out of it, and I just don't care anymore.

DAY 149

Today, we are sailing fast and mostly to the north, only making a little easting. I have chosen to sail up alongside the low, hoping to get a sling-shot effect over the top of it in favorable winds.

At least, today, there is no rain, and I work below removing more mold from all surface areas, as God knows Debbie won't want to sleep on a moldy boat.

My food supplies are dwindling, as is my waistline. I have but two cereal breakfasts left and no more Spam to go with the hot cakes to make my Hawaiian breakfast. I have 6 packages of cookies left, with four cookies in each one. The propane is a question mark, and I just pray it makes it. "Sun coffee" anyone? I soon will have to get creative with the breakfasts, like Top Ramen with a can of tuna and a can of vegetables in it. I have plenty of those ingredients and lots of canned fruit, as well as a piece of chocolate bar for each of the remaining days.

DAY 150

Wow, 5 months at sea and still 5000+ NM to go! We are now on top of the low and hauling ass in the right direction. Soon, our next big challenge is getting around the bottom of the very large South Pacific high, as this can be tricky for three reasons:

First: It can move faster than we can.

Second: Often times, there are lows embedded in its west side, raising havoc with wind speed and directions.

Third: The Humboldt Current that runs up the coast of Chile can be a great asset or just plain dangerous. Should a high develop over the interior of Chile then move west onto the Pacific causing northern winds against this 2-knot current, I will have square waves formed directly in my path. This only happens occasionally, and I pray I have a bit of good luck there.

Now that I am further north, the world is a little fatter, and that is why my distance to the turn has decreased very little, but for now, at least, I am closer to Ecuador.

Somewhat traumatized by "Patches", the Jefe'.

DAY 151

Once again, "Sailors Run" is sailing fast along the course line. There is a shallow spot in the ocean out here, about a day away along our course line. It was reported by the Vessel Sophia Christianson in 1913 and is reported to be 30 feet deep. That seems strange, as all the rest of the ocean in this area is three miles deep. Oh well, we will skirt by this one.

Debbie's father passed away, and she was at the burial today, a very sad time for her. Debbie's father had served in the US Air force in the special security squadron and could speak seven different languages. He was an all-around good person and will be missed by those who knew him.

Days 141-160

Temperatures are now quite pleasant aboard Sailors Run, and the Ecuadorian vegetable oil is almost a liquid once again.

DAY 152

I awoke in the middle of the night to the sound of luffing sails and found I was about 60° off-course. I put on my foul weather gear and went topside. I disconnected the wind vane and gave the wheel a spin. I was shocked as I watched it spin like the wheel of fortune. Once again, a steering cable has failed. This sent a sense of fear through me, as I have yet to find the spare steering cables. You can only break these things so many times before you wonder if they are going to last long enough to get us back home. Pulling all the stuff out of the two outside lockers, tearing apart the steering system, and once again dropping the plate and pulleys off the bottom of the pedestal, I held the cables in my hand.

The break was in the cable that had not failed last time, but the other cable was showing some broken strands where it attaches to the chain, so it also needed to be remade. The repair took 8 hours. In the end, I had to drill out the chain to get a shackle to fit onto the end to lengthen it and make up for lost wire. I also used my Makita cutting wheel to cut the copper crimp off the cable, saving an extra 4 inches of much-needed cable length. These cables just barely went back on the quadrant. If this should happen again, I will have to resort to the emergency tiller and make changes to the lines on the wind vane to be able to steer the boat by the tiller.

DAY 153

Today is not too much different from yesterday, as once again, I was awakened by popping sails and being off-course. I roll out of my berth and climb out into the cockpit to find out what the Hell is going on now. It doesn't take too long to discover the servo rudder on the wind vane has broken off. Now, for the third time on this voyage, it is trailing in our wake behind the boat.

This will not be an easy fix, as the winds have risen to 30 knots, gusting 40. The mizzen must be dropped, as well as the small portion of "Patches" that is still flying, rolled in on the furler. Once this is completed, we are under staysail alone with 15-20 foot seas. Heaving-to^{xiv} is not a safe option in these steep breaking seas. Instead, I play with the balance of the boat and eventually get her sailing just a little downwind. She seems to be nearly sailing herself, allowing me to hang off the back of the boat and get the remaining piece of the breakaway tube out of the kick-up hinge joint, where the servo rudder bolts into it. I make a new piece and bolt the servo rudder back into the hinge joint, and after just 4 hours of precarious goings on, we are being steered by the wind-vane once again, on course at good speed.

Dreaming of sitting with Debbie on a white sandy beach under a parasol and sipping on an ice-cold beer, The Jefe'.

DAY 154

Today, the sailing was primarily under light wind conditions. I came across a fleet of commercial fishing boats and was contacted by Paul aboard "Seven Daughters", registered out of Haines, Alaska. They were fishing for albacore tuna, and Paul reported the fishing was slow yet slightly better than last year. He said, once they get 600 fish, they head for Tahiti for fuel then up to Vancouver, Canada, where they spend the off-season.

On this night, the sky was so clear that it looked like you could stand on deck and pick the stars out of the heavens above.

DAY 155

Today, I find myself studying the pilot charts, as I have become somewhat apprehensive about my planned easternmost point, where I had intended to turn north. The reason being, I'm late getting here, later than I had hoped, and the fall weather can be pretty unpredictable off the coast of Chile at 45° south and 85° west. I also must admit that I'm suffering a bit from battle fatigue and figure, if I'm going to deal with the elements, I would rather do it in warmer waters. I decide to go over the high or thru it, rather than sail under and around. This route will be slightly shorter and most likely no faster, but I feel safer doing this, given the time of year. I will still have adequate rhumb line mileage for a credited circumnavigation.

DAY 156

Sailing fast today close on the wind, with "Patches" rolled out just 10%, reefed main, reefed mizzen, and full staysail. The reason Patches is only 10% out is that she has three tears buried on the furled portion of the sail. I need a nice day and the desire to get her patched, and neither is in my midst at this time. "Patches," however, has become famous, and here is a song that was written about her by Liz Wilder, a follower of the adventure:

> *If you're happy and you know it, Patch it there!*
>
> *If you're sailing and you know it, Patch it here!*
>
> *If you're happy that you're sailing, and you know it needed Patching, then you just Patch it e.v.e.r.y.w.h.e.r.e.! ha-ha.*

Yes, happy that I'm sailing, and yes, I will no doubt be patching it everywhere.

DAY 157

Today, we started with light winds that filled in late in the afternoon, and we are currently sailing fast.

I received a most welcome email from Debbie. Once again, she has stepped up to be part of Team Sailors Run and agreed to yet another off-shore passage. We will depart Bahía, Ecuador in early November, sailing the Clipper Route to Barra De Navidad, Mexico, a passage of 2100 NM. It should take about 17 days.

Now, my immediate concerns are the two lows that I must deal with here in the Roaring 40s. One is already bringing me NW winds, so I will try to get the most easting as possible and slip a little to the north while trying to outrun the second low that is gradually overtaking me. It should hit by the 10th. This low is predicted to intensify rapidly and could end up right on top of us, pounding us with headwinds to 40+ knots. This is never a good feeling. For now, we just haul ass to the ENE and pray it drops in just behind us. You know what they say; if you can't run with the Big Dogs, you best just stay on the porch!

DAY 158

Today finds us still sailing fast with warm winds from the NW. It's so warm that I'm only wearing one set of long underwear on the bottom with shorts on top of them and double long underwear on top with a tee shirt. I'm still eating pancakes every other day with fruit and my special Top Ramen and tuna breakfast with fruit on the other days. There is no lunch, making that easy. Dinner is either chicken, spaghetti, and vegetables, or chicken, potatoes, and vegetables, or rice, chicken, and vegetables. I must admit my cooking skills are improving, as now the instant potatoes are coming out thicker than the gravy for a change. I do still get a small piece of chocolate for a treat each day and, for a little longer, a cup of cocoa in the evenings.

Those who have been following me by my Spot locator haven't been getting my position updates lately, as I'm in a remote part of the Pacific where there is no Spot coverage. I will however continue to set it out once a day until I hear from someone that it is being picked up again. After that, I will put it out twice a day. The reception should kick back in around 120° longitude.

DAY 159

Current Stats
Position
Lat. 41°19'S / Long. 131°52'W
Weather
Barometer = 1010 mb. -- Wind = 7-15 kts. - - Temp = 66°-71°
Seas
6-8 ft.

Distance
24 hr. run = 140 NM
Miles sailed last three days = 448 NM
Total miles sailed so far = 20,645 NM
Miles left to go to turn North = 978 NM

Top speed so far
14.1 kts.

Winds today are westerly and much lighter. Last night was another one of those nights when the sky looked like a bowl of diamonds.

It has been suggested to me by our good friends Cal & Elly, formerly from the yacht "Desperado", that I should harvest the gooseneck barnacles hanging on my stern. They are considered a delicacy in Europe and going for about 200 dollars a plate. They say they taste somewhere between clams and lobster. I'm thinking about doing it but have yet to devise a way to scrape them off and catch them at the same time. They are close to the water; possibly, a dust pan might work!

I'm still ahead of the low, but the winds are going light, much like the calm before the Storm.

Running and Scared Skinny, the Jefe'.

The Jefe'

DAY 160

Today is a cloudy day with light WNW winds, and early in the day, the barometer remains steady at 1010 mb. I'm waiting for the once fast-moving low, previously moving at 30 knots and coming down from the NW. It now appears to be slowing down to 15 knots and will be passing just above me or on top of me. I must admit this reminds me of when I was in the 6th grade and had shinned a kid while playing soccer during first recess. He challenged me to a fight after school, and I had agreed to meet him in one corner of the field out behind the school. Well, all day long, I watched the clock. It must have been every half hour that I fought this kid in my mind over and over again. At last, the final school bell rang, and my buddy and I went to the far corner of the field to wait for the kid. Wouldn't you know it? He never showed up. That was alright with me, as it must have also been with him, as he never came looking for me again.

Now, once again, I find myself watching the clock and the barometer for the fight that is yet to come. I know I must tack to the north when the 30 knot east winds arrive, but for now, it is purely a waiting game.

At last, "Patches" is back together after 23 days of sewing.

Steering cables fail for the second time; no easy repair at sea.

Short on water, I tried making my own distiller, no luck!

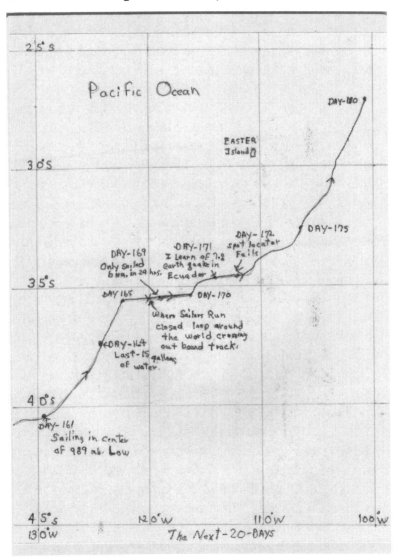

25°S

Pacific Ocean

DAY-180

EASTER
Island

30°S

DAY-175

DAY-169
Only sailed
6 nm. in 24 hrs.

DAY-171
I learn of 7.8
earth quake in
Ecuador

DAY-172
spot locator
Fails

35°S

DAY 165

DAY-170

When Sailors Run
closed loop around
the world crossing
out bound track.

DAY-164
Last-15 gallons
of water.

40°S

DAY-161
Sailing in center
of 989 mb. Low

45°S

130°W   120°W   110°W   100°W

The Next-20-DAYS

DAY 161

The day of reckoning is upon us as the winds steadily build, and the barometer plunges towards the bottom. It was just after dinner that my course started heading more to the south, and with the rising winds, I decided to drop the mainsail. I tacked over on to the starboard tack, now pounding to weather on a heading of 345°, giving up progress to the east.

The seas are rising 10-12 feet, and Sailors Run bashes headlong into them. Sometimes, I think an offshore cruising yacht should have a Tums dispenser both fore and aft! Now, I wonder, have I tacked too soon, giving up hard-earned miles, and how long will I have to continue on this tack? After just 30 minutes, the winds are blowing 30 knots, and after one hour, they are gusting over 40 knots. Even though it is dark and time to sleep, the Jefe' gets none. I squirm in my bunk, the safest place in bad weather, and wonder, by heading directly into this low, what kind of Pandora's box might I have opened?

Sailors Run has been my war horse so many times on this voyage. I feel my stomach muscles tense as she vaults off a huge wave and comes crashing down into the face of the next one. The mast shudders, and the entire hull vibrates. I wonder just how many times she can withstand this brutal punishment. I question myself: is there not something I can do to ease Sailors Run's struggle? After two hours, we are sailing due north and sometimes making 20-degrees of easting. I'm actually gaining some ground but at what seems like a huge risk of catastrophic failure in the deteriorating conditions. I run through the abandon-ship drill in my mind: May Day, Get out quick bag, Gumby suit [full immersion suit], deploy life raft.

After being launched off one particularly large wave where we grabbed a lot of air and crashed into the trough, slamming me down hard on my berth then sending a horrendous shuddering throughout the boat, I finally said, "That's it!" I rolled out of my berth and suited up to go topside. Once in the cockpit, I hurriedly altered our course away from the wind and waves by about 10 degrees. I can't fall off too much for fear of taking a large breaking wave on the beam and getting knocked down, or worse, rolled all the way over.

Once safely below decks, I check the barometer, and it is now reading 990 mb. We are obviously beating through the squall-filled outer-eye wall of the low. I wonder how long it will take to reach the core of the low. This started about 6 p.m., and at 2 a.m., suddenly, the wind appears to have stopped and all is quiet below. I go topside to see what is going on and find that we are back-winded in a moderate 17 knot breeze from the North. I trim in the sails as they should be and reset the wind-vane. We are now sailing almost due east in a nice breeze. The confused seas slam into us from all directions, but they are smaller seas, and Sailors Run takes them in stride.

We are now sailing inside the low, and the barometer is reading 986 mb. The low is moving over us, and I wonder how long before the back of the low's eye wall will overtake us. Soon, I collapse into a deep sleep.

DAY 162

After four hours, its 10 a.m. My eyes pop open, and I find we are sailing along nicely to the east with the barometer still at 986 mb. Suddenly, at 3 p.m., our world changes as the back wall strikes us and the winds go to the SW at 30-40+ knots. The mizzen comes down, and we sail on a broad reach under staysail alone, hitting 7 knots at times.

The seas are higher now, reaching 20 feet. This happens because, in the Southern Ocean, there is almost always a SW swell running 6-10 feet, and when you apply 40 knots of wind to those swells, they grow rapidly into storm force seas. Sailors Run's cockpit is filled several times by waves breaking over the stern, and several rogue waves strike us on the beam, forcing small amounts of water below decks at times. When Sailors

The Jefe'

Run runs before these following seas, it remains fairly comfortable below decks, and sometimes, I can actually sleep. Riding out the blow! The Jefe'.

DAY 163

The barometer is rising, and soon, the winds begin coming down. Many hours later, the seas also drop as I breathe a sigh of relief. I put the mizzen back up, and several hours later, in 20 knots of breeze, I hoist the mainsail to keep up my speed.

Today is Sunday, and I always run the engine 15 minutes in neutral to circulate the oil and dry the moisture out of the engine. When I go out in the cockpit to shut down the engine, I'm greeted by a strange, rather musical sound, like someone playing the comb with wax paper on it. I look over the stern at the exhaust water, and there is just a trickle coming out; the exhaust without water is making the music. I immediately shut down the engine and soon realize my mistake. I share this with you, as it might save you problems in the future. Since I was sailing well-heeled-over and waves on the beam were rolling me over even further, at times, I was sucking air instead of water into the engine thru-hull fitting. This smoked the rubber impeller on the raw water pump, which needs the water for cooling and lubrication. This has never happened before, but I should have realized it could. Fortunately, I have spare impellers, and it is an easy fix.

DAY 164

We have a drought aboard Sailors Run, and now, our reservoir is down to the last 15 gallons of water. We still have about three weeks to go, and I might be able to make it. I still have the hand-operated water maker that I have been advised not to use because I will end up looking like Popeye! Well, that might not be so bad after all. My Hash Harrier (runners group) name that I was given in Samoa is Popeye.

Days 161-180

There is yet another low that has formed NW of me and headed my way. This one I do believe will pass astern but will impede my progress by hitting me with 25+ Knot winds from the NE, forcing me to the SE.

DAY 165

Today, I headed into what was going to be a very productive day. First, I replaced the impeller on the engine and had a bit of trouble as my liquid gasket material in the tube had set-up solid. I made do by using the inflatable dinghy glue for the gasket material, and it seemed to work.

Next on my list was Patches. I decided, since it was a nice day, to bring her down and do the three needed patches. This project went sideways on me from the get-go. The halyard jammed in the mast where it entered because the outer jacket on the line had chafed through and bunched up causing the jam. The sail won't come down without me going up in the bosun's chair, cutting away the excess jacket, and taping it down so it can enter the mast. Since the last time I patched Patches and then put her up, only to see another two-foot tear in just 15 minutes, I have a hard time going through all that this repair will require. For now, it's back to using Patches rolled out at 10-15%. Possibly, if I get stuck in the center of a high, I will be more motivated. With the genoa rolled in, it was safe to take the strain off the failing halyard, thereby reducing the likelihood of it chafing through it.

I have changed our distance to go from the turn north to the finish line at Bahía. I still need to get east for weather reasons and will be trying to do that, but lately, these lows have been forcing me north at times. It comes down to a chess game where you try to anticipate the weather's next move, so you can place your vessel in the right part of the ocean. This can be very frustrating, and sometimes, very little forward progress is made.

The Jefe'

"Eenie, meenie, miney moe", which in the Hell way should the Jefe' go?

DAY 166

Today, we went over on the port tack, taking us to the SE, where hopefully winds from the low will allow us to sail to the east.

I have eaten the last of the popcorn and drank my last cup of cocoa. I can substitute tea for the cocoa, but there is nothing for the popcorn. The one good thing about me eating my way to the bottom of all our provisions is that all the new stuff I replace this with will be good for several years down the road.

The ocean is warming up around us, and the warm, moist air coming down from the tropics seems so thick you could cut it with a knife.

Debbie is packing her bags. In those bags will be our new refrigeration system and a few other goodies for the boat.

Now, with just a little over 3000nm to go, all I have to do is sail a distance across the Pacific equal to the size of the United States!

DAY 167

I'm currently closing in on my outward-bound track and should be crossing that tomorrow. The low that showed in the weather info that would be overtaking me, apparently has gone someplace else, and hopefully, the sailing will be much better than yesterday.

It's truly amazing how my cooking skills are coming along. Take my gravy, for instance. I switched from using two cups of flour to two tablespoons. Now, the gravy just flows over whatever you put it on, whereas before, you could have laid bricks with it. Also, making gravy in a frying pan is never a good idea when pounding to weather unless the stove and cabin sole need oiling. I now need ski poles to stay at the stove when heeled over.

DAY 168

Current Stats

Position
Lat. 36°20'S / Long. 119°09'W

Weather
Barometer = 1009 mb. -- Wind = 3-40 kts. - - Temp = 73°-73°

Seas
8-18 ft.

Distance
24 hr. run = 99 NM
Miles sailed last three days = 205 NM
Total miles sailed so far = 21,508 NM
Distance left to go to the finish line = 3032 NM

Top speed so far
14.1 kts.

Today, winds are gusting over 40 knots, and I have had to go to the staysail and run off for a while until winds settle back down.

Today is another milestone of the voyage. After 167 days and 8 hours, we have crossed over our out-bound route, completing our loop around the globe. Now, it is just a matter of sailing to the finish line of Bahía Caraquez, Ecuador, and who knows how long that might take?

In search of favorable winds, the Jefe'.

DAY 169

This morning finds Sailors Run becalmed, and it starts to pour rain. I suit up and quickly get on deck, plugging up the scuppers to trap the rain. I scoop up the puddled water, managing to get a much-needed 15 gallons into the starboard tank. Obtaining this water lets me breathe a little easier, as now, I possibly have enough to get to Bahía.

The Jefe'

It appears I have a 0.7 knot counter-current pushing us to the west, and we stay becalmed for twenty hours before the winds start to fill in from the north. The result is the worst day of the trip so far, netting only 6 nautical miles. This very dismal performance was only slightly offset by the water I had collected, and at this rate, it will take 503 more days to get to Bahía... Hmmmmmm!

I think this is when you are supposed to start off-loading excess weight. In the old sailing days, it was the horses that went. I can't seem to find any damn horses, so pray for wind as a birthday gift for tomorrow.

DAY 170—HAPPY BIRTHDAY TO ME

Today is another milestone in my life, as on April 17th, 2016, I sail into my 70th year, and I did get my present of plenty of wind to sail with. When I think of my age and what I'm doing, I have to reflect upon my mentor, Clarence Plotts. I met Clarence while studying with the Tacoma Power Squadron, soaking up all I could about navigation, seamanship, and sailing. Clarence taught the sailing course, and he saw the keen interest I displayed for sailing. One thing led to another, and I ended up racing with Clarence aboard his beloved boat "Pinocchio" for three years, and we kicked ass. Clarence raced until he was 90 years old, and at age 92, I helped him sail Pinocchio to Seattle to put her up for sale.

I remember asking Clarence what he would do now. He said he was just about done and wouldn't last Long. Clarence died on his 93rd birthday, but I can assure you, he was very much alive and lived life to the fullest for at least 92 of those years.

DAY 171

Debbie and I are both devastated by the catastrophic damage caused by the 7.8-magnitude earthquake in Ecuador. Our hearts and prayers go out to the Ecuadorian people in their struggle to survive, as they start the rebuilding process. We have many friends in Bahía Caraquez, and fortunately, we believe they have all survived. Some are homeless and living at the college with many other people from their area. We are gradually starting to get the picture as to the extent of the damage to homes, buildings, and businesses where people might have been employed. Phone lines are down, and power is out in many areas. Because the whole west coast is affected, recovery will be slow, and resources are in short supply locally.

For me and Sailors Run, it feels much like being on a space mission where you are returning to earth, and when you get back, it somehow looks very different from when you left. Debbie and I have not yet been able to contact Tripp, the marina owner, and are not even sure there is an open channel to re-enter the river. We do know Tripp, Maye, and daughter Francheska are OK. We have no doubt they are dealing with the disaster and taking care of priorities.

So, for now, I sail on for Bahía, and by the time I arrive, I will have boots on the ground, Debbie. Who knows? I might see her out there shoveling the channel at low tide, so I can get in! We hoped to leave the boat there and fly home, but we're not sure there is a "there" anymore!

I will be out of food, water, and propane by then. Worst case, I will have to provision off-shore and sail for Peru or the Marquesas, as I don't like the lightning in Panama or the Hurricanes off Mexico in the summer.

So, as for that big planned celebration, it doesn't look real promising, but I am sure, like most things, it will somehow all work out just fine.

Hmmmmmm, which way to steer?

DAY 172

Today, I sailed on into dying winds that, by the end of the day, were nearly nonexistent.

The Jefe'

It's strange how things happen, as today, both my Spot locator device and my outside GPS started acting up. The Spot no longer has the right light configuration when you turn it on and seems to have failed. The GPS's hot power terminal for the external power source has corroded away and now requires new batteries every 24 hours. Fortunately, they are double A batteries, and I have a bunch of them. These two pieces of electronic equipment are the 4th and 5th pieces of electronic equipment to have failed due to the harsh Southern Ocean environment.

DAY 173

The winds are staying light as yet another low forms right on top of us. This area seems to be the nurturing source where the warm, moist winds coming down from the north tend to start circulating over these cooler waters, forming into low pressure systems that move off to the south-east. This becomes the challenge to any sailor out on the open ocean, which is to marry the forces of nature to his sailing vessel into a harmonious relationship that powers them together across the great expanses of vast oceans.

One can only find peace of mind far out on the ocean by being confident in the seaworthiness of his vessel, the knowledge and experience that he, the skipper, always has a plan to deal with whatever nature brings his way next.

DAY 174

Today, the winds are increasing and from a direction that is propelling us along on a favorable course. We have been pounding to weather for the last week, having to stay close to the winds of varying strengths to gain distance towards our destination.

Debbie just informed me that she read in May 2016 *Latitude 38* that I'm the oldest American to circumnavigate via the 5 Great Capes. The oldest person in the world to do it was a

Japanese sailor, Minoru Saito, 71 years old, on a 50-footer in 2004-5. The oldest woman is British sailor, Jean Socrates, 70 years young, on a 38-foot boat just a year or two ago. Now, this is a great honor, but I was kind of hoping to be the hottest guy to solo the 5-Great Capes. Debbie says I am! HA HA! Well, I just hope this feat entitles me to 50% off on everything it's going to take to put Humpty Dumpty [Sailors Run] back together again.

Come on "Finish Line". Anxiously looking forward to the end!

DAY 175

Once again, Sailors Run is put to the test, pounding hard to weather in very rough seas under reefed mizzen, staysail, and a tiny bit of Patches. The SW swell at 10 feet collides with the wind waves that are up to 15 feet from the North, causing me to have to bang and crash forward towards my destination. I'm hoping to pick up the SE trades in about 3 days and leave the worst weather in our wake astern.

We are still sailing on into uncertainty, as there is no word back from Tripp Martin at the marina as to whether the channel into Bahía is open. Debbie is doing all she can to get this info. She heard the channel has moved but not if it is still navigable.

DAY 176

Today, the sailing is great, and the winds, as well as the seas, are down a little.

I'm down to my last big chocolate bar, and they will be greatly missed; however, I have a big bag of chocolate chips that will pick up some of the slack in the chocolate department. I believe I only have five more Top Ramen breakfasts before I go to pancakes every day. Dinners seem to be holding out for now.

The Jefe'

I awoke about 5 a.m. to screeching winds. A very powerful squall was upon us, somewhere in the 50-knot range, and the reefed main needed to come down. I struggled to get clear of my berth on the port side, as Sailors Run was pinned down hard on her side. It seemed like forever to get the foulies and boots on before clambering on deck. I clipped in and inched forward with spray and waves crashing about. Once at the mast, I grabbed the halyard to the main, let it fly, and hauled down the sail, while clinging to the mast. These very wild conditions seemed to be trying to pitch me off the boat.

It wasn't until early the next morning that I discovered the strap that holds the double mainsheet block had popped off one of the 5/16" rivets, separating it from one of the two 4-wheel slides that run on the main sheet track. I made a temporary fix with a small bolt and reattached the strap. I believe this should hold until I get in.

DAY 177

After the big squall, the winds died down to where we were eventually becalmed for 4 hours. We rocked and rolled in the cross seas, forcing me to reduce sail, thereby reducing the flogging. Eventually, the winds slowly filled in, and we were off once again, homeward bound.

I had really great news on the Sail-Mail⁽ᵛ⁾ last night. The email was from Tripp Martin, congratulating me on the circumnavigation and letting me know they are waiting for my arrival in Bahía, and YES, not only is the channel open, but it now appears to be one meter deeper. Tripp is doing all he can to take care of the cruisers, and he expects the power, as well as the internet service, to be back on at Puerto Amistad in the next couple of days. Now, I have to share with you, I breathed a huge sigh of relief upon hearing this news. Trying to keep it together and complete this odyssey.

DAY 178

Sailing fast today, dropping down the mizzen when the winds exceed 25 knots to maintain a better course downwind.

Before I left on this voyage, my friend John was looking at all the canned goods that I was taking, and he said, "You better make sure you have two can openers." I already had one nice one I had paid 9 dollars for, so I picked up a second cheap one in Ecuador for $1.50 and figured I was set. Now, after nearly 6 months and many cans later, neither of those two can openers work. Although it should be said, the cheap can opener opened twice as many cans as the expensive one. Fortunately, I have two Leatherman multipurpose tools—you know, the ones with pliers, knife blades, saws, files etc. The can openers on those tools are tough and work perfectly every time with no moving parts except your muscles.

DAY 179

Today is a nice sunny day with much lighter winds, and the thermometer actually hit 86°F. I used to believe 75° was the perfect temperature, but after spending so many years in the little latitudes and out on the water, I now believe 86° is perfect.

With approximately 2 weeks left to go, I must begin to prepare myself for re-entry into a more complex life with stimuli coming from many different directions then watch as the oneness of the solo sailor slowly vanishes, left once again out upon the sea.

I must now be especially cautious and aware. I must not let my guard down, as I'm not yet there. I must wait until I'm safely moored inside, upon the Rio Chone River, before finally letting my guard down.

This particular voyage is one huge stream of consciousness that I'm sure will linger in my mind forever. All my previous adventures will pale in comparison to this one, and I doubt I will ever do anything to compare to it in either my future sailing or otherwise. I am truly glad I have had the opportunity to share this experience with many others and hope it will possibly, in some way, help them to step up and take on their next big adventure.

DAY 180

Current Stats
Position
Lat. 27°12'S / Long. 100°51'W

Weather
Barometer = 1005 mb. -- Wind = 6-10 kts. - - Temp = 73°-75°

Seas
6-10 ft.

Distance
24 hr. run = 75 NM
Miles sailed last three days = 325 NM
Total miles sailed so far = 22,792 NM
Distance left to finish at Bahia = 1976 NM

Top speed so far
14.1 kts.

The winds seem to be getting lighter. I knew this route might not be the fastest, but I have opted for the safer route. We have been flying the spinnaker for the past 17 hours, and the winds have stayed light.

A very good friend of mine, Wayne, asked me what food I missed the most. I started thinking about it and was drooling by the time I was done. One food wasn't enough at this point, so I decided, if I had my choice, my special meal, whether it is upon my arrival to Bahía Caraquez or before they hang or shoot me, would go like this: Nice greasy fried chicken, homemade French fries with tartar sauce, tossed green salad with blue cheese dressing, a grape float of ice cream and grape pop. Now that is not dessert, as that would be a couple of rum and cokes with Debbie, and of course, there is nothing wrong with having dessert first!

Trying to get there, the Jefe'.

Historical Museum in shambles in Bahia.

Earthquake damage in Bahia Caraquez, Ecuador.

The new school in Bahia was a total loss.

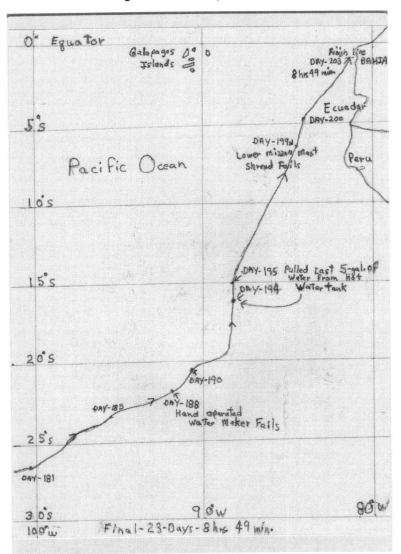

0° Equator

Galapagos Islands

0

Finish Line
DAY-203 ↗ BAHIA
8 hrs 49 min

Ecuador
DAY-200

5°s

Pacific Ocean

DAY-199N
Lower mizzen mast
Shroud Fails

Peru

10°s

15°s

DAY-195 Pulled Last 5-gal. of
Water From Hot
DAY-194   Water Tank

20°s

DAY-190

DAY-185   DAY-188
Hand operated
Water Maker Fails

25°s

DAY-181

30°s
100°w

90°w

80°w

Final-23-Days-8 hrs 49 min.

DAY 181

Today, I find myself staring at my weather information, rubbing my head and trying to figure out how to keep Sailors Run moving. It seems the highs and lows are forming right where I am, and the pressure in the lows is the same as the pressure in the highs. I honestly don't know how they know whether they are a high or a low! I can only guess it depends upon which way they spin first, as here, highs rotate counterclockwise and lows rotate clockwise. The thing I know for sure is there is very little wind from any direction, making progress for Sailors Run nearly impossible.

My biggest concern right now is that, when Debbie gets to Bahía Caraquez, she will be sleeping outside, as many of our friends cannot enter their homes until they are inspected and determined to be safe by the government. With the many magnitude 4-6 aftershocks they are having, most people are content to be outside. Fortunately, the temperature is normally in the 80s day and night with very little rain.

Debbie has purchased a sleeping bag and is gearing up for the conditions that await her. I, on the other hand, feel pressed to get there and provide shelter for her.

DAY 182

Today, I spent 75% of the time becalmed, feeling frustrated and needing to get moving. It is once again time for Patches to come down for more patches. Soon, I find myself aloft in the bosun's chair, swinging around on the end of the staysail halyard. It wasn't easy, but I finally managed to separate the outer jacket on the halyard that had been hanging up where it enters the mast. Once free, the jacket was pulled off, exposing 60 feet of core. I sewed the new replacement halyard to the core, pulled it into the mast, and reattached it to the genoa. Soon, Patches was down on deck, and I began the patching process. I only managed to get one 18-inch double patch completed before it got too late.

DAY 183

Once again, I find myself butt planted on the foredeck, sewing away on Patches. I install a second double patch, about 25 inches long and glued on two more small double patches with Hypalon dinghy glue. Soon, the sail is back up on the furle, and we must wait for a suitable breeze to sail with.

Someone recently asked me what I was going to do with Patches after the voyage. My first thought was a huge bonfire, where all my friends and I, wearing voodoo masks, dance around naked as Patches goes up in flames. Now that was my idea; another friend, Patty had a great idea. When I write the book about this epic adventure, I put a small piece of Patches in each of the first 10,000 copies sold, and that seems like a better idea. Now, I just have to figure out how to get my publisher to do that!

My canned chicken is all gone, and all that remains for the rest of the voyage is canned tuna, unless I catch something. My water supply is less than good. It seems, as I near the bottom of the tank, the salinity is going up. It is possible that some salt water was introduced into the tanks either from storm waves breaking on deck and being forced into the tanks through the air vents or from collecting water on a less than salt free deck. So now, it is time to pull out the hand operated water maker and pray that it works!

Feeling a little too salty, the Jefe'.

DAY 184

Today, I'm sailing close to the wind, pounding into 20-25 knots of breeze and pretty much on-course. Later in the morning, I found myself digging down into the get-out-quick bag, looking for the hand-operated water maker. Once I found it, I turned over the sealed plastic it was wrapped in and read a warning on the wrapper that said, "This Pur-06 water maker must be serviced annually by an authorized dealer". Hmm, let's see. I put it in the bag 17+ years ago, and now, I need it to make water today!

Conditions are pretty rough to make almost anything, but I decide the galley sink is the best place to set up this operation. I use a 2-gallon bucket to fetch salt water from over the side of the boat then place it in the sink. I drop the pick-up line from the water maker in the bucket and place the waste water line in the sink, where it can drain out. The product water goes into a 1-quart Gatorade bottle. Now, you must purge the unit, getting rid of the biocide preservative; that takes 80 strokes once you have water coming out of the product water tube.

My friend Eric warned me about this amazing piece of equipment and how much work they are, but until you actually experience it, it's hard to imagine. I pumped on the thing for an hour and had gone through at least 10 gallons of salt water and felt for sure I should have a quart of drinking water. However, that was not the case. What I did have was more like 5-6 ounces of drinkable water. This equates to 7 hours of pumping just for the water to make a pot of coffee. Hmmmm, that salty water in the tank is starting to taste not so bad after all. You know, just add more sugar. I decided I would make half my coffee water with the water maker and get the rest from the salty stuff in the tank.

DAY 185

Once again, great sailing today, and I saw the first cargo ship since New Zealand. It showed up on the A.I.S., crossing our bow some 17 NM ahead of us. The ship appeared to be coming from Chile headed west.

Faced with a water shortage onboard, you start thinking about things differently, such as, when I heat up vegetables for dinner, I no longer drain the vegetables. Instead, I drink that extra liquid that comes in each can. I do the same with any other liquids or juices, like the canned fruit. I also have 5 liters of apple and peach juice that I have held back on drinking for just such an occasion. I will ration these out over the remainder of the voyage. I have 3 quarts of water in the get-out-quick bag that I can also use to help with the fresh water for coffee. My friends Brent & Susan also reminded me that there should be several gallons of water in my hot water tank. I can get at that by using my Hooka compressor to blow all the water out of the lines, as well as the tank.

Today, Debbie flies out, headed for Bahía Caraquez, Ecuador. I know she has a sleeping bag, but I don't believe she has a tent. I can only hope, if it rains, she has enough sense to sleep under a bridge by a support column. Just kidding, I hope.

DAY 186

Great sailing today under trade wind clouds and blue skies. I have about 15 knots of breeze. I have not yet reached the SE trades. The high that helps fuel the trades is just NE of me. It looks like I will have to sail through a portion of the center to get into those winds that I will use to drive me to Bahía.

Getting saltier by the day, the Jefe'.

DAY 187

The winds diminished throughout the day, and I sail through the night at 2 knots under the star-filled heavens above. We are now so close to the SE-Trade Winds that I can almost taste them. They are about 100 NM to the North of us.

It's amazing to me how much I dwell on my water situation now that it is in short supply. Water is something we take for granted normally. Tomorrow, I will start pumping that water maker for two hours instead of only one.

It has been suggested by Debbie and Al, formerly from the yacht Different Worlds, that I should pass on the coffee, as it is a diuretic, and just drink the water. I just might have to do that. Can you believe it? First, I had to give up the alcohol, then variety in the foods I get to eat, and now give up coffee?

Pretty soon, there will be no difference between being alive and dead.

DAY 188

Today, my water-making came to a screeching halt as the Pur-06 hand operated water maker quit putting out product water. I dug around and found the alkaline treatment chemicals used for cleaning the membrane of the water maker. Hopefully, tomorrow we will be back in business.

We are ghosting along in very light airs, and thankfully, we are getting 110% out of Patches, or we would not be moving at all. Taking full advantage of the calm conditions, I hoisted myself up the main mast in the bosun's chair and replaced the flag halyard at the starboard spreader; it had parted early on. I also dragged the 60 lb. CQR anchor out of the aft locker and secured it on the bow roller, where it normally rides under more normal sailing conditions. The anchor chain I will leave stowed below amidships until we get a little closer to our destination, keeping that weight out of the forward chain locker as long as I can.

I should mention Debbie is in Bahía, and they are ready for me to get there!

DAY 189

After a miserable sailing performance yesterday, I start today becalmed. I pull my weather information via the single sideband radio and feel disheartened. It appears the center of the high is moving to the north with us, keeping the trade winds just out of reach of Sailors Run and crew. This pattern seems to continue over the next three days.

By mid-morning, things have deteriorated even further aboard Sailors Run as the alkaline treatment has yielded no results on the water maker, and it appears to be useless. I now take inventory of my situation.

I have:

1-1/2 liters of good fresh water left.

3-1/4 liters of fruit juice.

20 cans of various vegetables containing water.

10 large cans of a variety of fruits: peaches, fruit cocktail, and pineapple.

28 cans of tuna.

The rest of the provisions are: rice, flour, and pasta, most of which require water to make. I plan to eat just the tuna, vegetables, and fruit, plus pancakes for breakfast every day.

I still have 1400 miles to go, and once in the trades, I will move fast, but for now, I'm just praying for wind, as rain in this area is pretty unlikely. I cannot accept any help or take on any water or provisions before crossing the finish line at Bahía; those are the rules.

Rain dancing in prayer, the Jefe'.

DAY 190

Winds have piped up a little today yet are still very light. The good thing is I can almost steer the desired course, a big improvement over yesterday.

I have received many great ideas from those out there who are following me on how to help diminish my water shortage problem. I will name a few I think could be beneficial to someone in my situation.

1. A quick and easy one is to use a 4-quart sauce pan on your stove with a cup secured in the middle of it and salt water poured into and around the cup but not over the cup. Then place the pot lid upside down on the pan and boil the salt water. The steam condensing on the lid will run down to the knob and drip into the cup.

2. Another great idea is take your pressure cooker and, either by removing a pop up or drilling a hole in the top, attach a copper tube. Then coil it as a condenser, so the steam is cooled and converted to fresh water that runs out the end of

the tube. A plastic tube could be substituted for copper as long as it didn't taint the taste of the water.

3. A solar still. Take a pop or beer can with the top cut off and fill it with sea water. Then take a 2-liter plastic pop bottle with the top on and cut a hole in the bottom for the can. Next, roll up the bottom of the pop bottle inside, creating a trough around the inside of the bottle and then just set it in the sun. It's supposed to work.

4. Use a hand-operated water maker to pump the salty tainted water in the tank through the water maker. This should yield more fresh water quicker; save the discharge water for other cleaning uses.

Of course, the first two ideas require that you have enough propane to boil the water. I'm not sure I do, but as a last resort, I will give it a go. The water maker idea is a good one, but my water maker refuses to produce any product water from any source at this time.

John, from the yacht Nakia, reminded me that the hot water tank has a back-flow preventer on the bottom of it, and the only real way to get the water out of the tank is to remove that back-flow device. So, I logged all that good info. I also checked the specifications on my life raft, and there are 3 liters of 17-year-old water inside it, which could be used if need be; actually, now that I think of it, all water is much older than that.

DAY 191

Today, winds are up just a little, and I'm able to sail on-course.

I decided to build a 6-volt battery for my water salinity tester, as the factory battery died, and I didn't have a replacement. I taped 4 AA batteries into a bundle, placing every other one + end up. On the bottom of the battery pack, I soldered two separate parallel bare copper wires connecting the negative ends of two batteries to the positive ends of the other two batteries, creating two 3-volt batteries. On top of the battery bundle, I connected the negative of one three-volt battery to the positive of the other one, and that gave me 6 volts at the two remaining terminals. I soldered two wires onto those, connected them in the meter where the normal 6-volt battery would hook up and, of course, the meter turned on. This enabled me to fill a cup with the salty water from my tank and read the salinity. According to my "Pur" water maker manual, any product water over 1500 parts per million should be discarded. My meter read 1480 parts per million, making the water barely drinkable. So, for now, I'm still using the tank water and drinking my coffee with extra sugar. I feel much relieved to have this additional water. We will see how long it lasts.

DAY 192

Current Stats

Position
Lat. 17°43'S / Long. 88°23'W

Weather
Barometer = 1010 mb. -- Wind = 8-12 kts. - - Temp = 75°-78°

Seas
4-6 ft.

Distance
24 hr. run = 131 NM
Miles sailed last three days = 301 NM
Total miles sailed so far = 23,801 NM
Distance left to finish at Bahia = 1124 NM

Top speed so far
14.1 kts.

Sailing along nicely and picking up a favorable current, it is most likely the outer edge of the Humboldt Current. I can see the trade winds getting closer and should start to get into them within 24 hours. First, I have to pass through the transitional area where I will be slowed for at least 12 hours before I can get moving once again.

The Jefe'

Debbie is reporting in from Bahía Caraqez, Ecuador, where she is sleeping in a 3-man tent out in the yard of our friend Dan's house. She says there are people sleeping in tents on the streets of Bahía. She also mentioned they tried opening the Tia store in the downtown section, and the people all went in and looted it. So now, it is closed until security is beefed up enough to reopen. Debbie says there are lots of soldiers on the streets, making things pretty safe. A few stores with lots of security are now open. There were deaths in Bahía when some large buildings collapsed. Tripp sold the marina. It is now open under new ownership and management, but most of the old employees are still there. The Puerto Amistad restaurant should also be open by the time I get there. Dan has become my official finisher, as his house overlooks the finish line.

The Ecuador earthquake is a pretty good example of what I alluded to several months before the earthquake happened. Hunger is our strongest driving force, and very few people are provisioned to last more than a few days before they become desperate and will take what they need at whatever risk. We should all learn from this example, as this was an unpredictable natural disaster, and they do happen in most places. It's hard when you know there is normally a store two blocks away, stuffed full of whatever you might want. Unfortunately, in an event like this, it could be gone when you really need it. At that point, the store becomes an illusion, and that is what I am talking about.

I had provisioned Sailors Run for approximately 7 months. When all those lockers were jammed to the tops with goods, it seemed almost ridiculous that I should take so much stuff, but now I'm down to just about the same place in my provisions as many of the people in Ecuador. From this perspective, it causes you to think sobering thoughts. Fortunately, I can see a light at the end of the tunnel.

Watching the light grow larger and brighter as the Jefe' gets saltier, day by day.

DAY 193

On this day, sailing is slow as we try to get clear of the center of the high.

We had a close encounter with a 120-foot Ecuadorian fishing vessel "Bandana" that set off the A.I.S. Alarm. I tried contacting the vessel on VHF-radio, as it appeared the 120-foot fishing vessel was bearing down on me. After several attempts, the skipper came back to me in broken English, assuring me there was no problem, and he was altering course. I used my best broken Spanish to let him know all was "muy bueno" with that. He chuckled into the microphone and passed ½ mile off my stern. What seemed pretty funny is that, as he passed behind me, there was a large school of tuna jumping out of the water off my port bow happily frolicking, swimming clear of both our vessels.

DAY 194

In the early morning hours, the winds remained light as I slowly moved forward, hoping to find the SE-Trades.

Today was the day I had hoped to avoid, as both water tanks are exhausted of all water, and only a fine fog ushered forth from the spigot in the galley sink. My next attempt at water recovery was to retrieve the water from the hot water tank. I pulled the high-pressure blow-off valve off an upper portion of the tank, and water began to bubble forth. I was using a funnel and two-liter bottles to collect the water. In the end, I had used many old two-liter pop bottles from my recycled plastic waste department. Once the water was below the level of the hole created by removing the blow off valve, I resorted to using the 06-Pur water maker as a pump to get at the remaining water that was down in the tank. Once the hand pump was sucking near the bottom of the tank, the water sud-

The Jefe'

denly appeared rusty, so I stopped and left the remainder behind. From the 6-gallon water tank, I was able to retrieve 5 gallons of salt-tainted water with readings of 1480 ppm to 1800 ppm on the salinity tester.

It was pointed out by friends of mine in the medical field that the law in the US requires drinking water to be less than 500 ppm, and in Mexico, it is required to be less than 750ppm. Possibly that is because, with all the Tequila they drink, their kidneys can handle more salt! They also recommended that I drink my urine, rather than the salty water, as it would be safer. I just have to say, if I was worried about safety, I would have *never* circumnavigated via the 5-great capes! So, after not too much deliberating about this, I have concluded that, since I have drunk no rum for over two months, my kidneys need a little adventure, and I hope for a week or so, they will see me through urine-free.

As dinner time rolled around, I figured I would combine one of the water recovery ideas with cooking. When I steamed the whole-grained brown rice, I had a cup placed in the center of the 4-quart pan and the lid turned upside down on the top. This allowed the steam to be diverted off the knob on the pot lid and into the cup. After 40 minutes of steaming the 1-cup of rice in 2.5 cups of water, my yield in the cup was 1.5 ounces of salt free water. That was not much, but I dumped it into the coffee pot to reduce the salinity on my next batch of coffee.

DAY 195

Still no trade winds, although for about 4 hours, the winds were up a little, and we were moving pretty well.

Last night, some showers came our way, and I set about trapping water on deck, but by the time I was set up, the rains stopped. At least I have clean decks and sails for the next shower if it comes.

The past two mornings, I have found flying fish on deck, usually a good sign for improved fishing. I have had little luck fishing, and I believe this is mainly because the boat is seldom moving fast enough to cause the lures to be effective.

I saw yet another cargo ship on the A.I.S. last evening, but it never came any closer than 25 miles. It appeared to be headed in the direction of Callow, Peru, the largest port on the west side of South America.

This evening, I watched as the sun dipped below the horizon and was treated to the most magnificent "green flash" I have yet to see. I believe, because I stepped up on the coaming edge around the cockpit just as it started to happen and then the boat rose up on a wave, it caused the green flash to last for a full 3-seconds. This was a real "ooh-ah-ooh" event, followed by a most beautiful sunset. I guess there are still more wonderful things for me to experience on this voyage. Maybe King Neptune and the Mayan wind God Chau-Xib-Chac, pronounced Quaxicatle, have teamed up to keep Sailors Run and crew out here just a little longer.

Still ghosting along in the Pacific, the Jefe'.

DAY 196

The SE trade winds have begun to fill in at last. Now, I pray Patches will hold together in the building trade winds for this final dash to the finish.

Last evening, I was treated to another amazing green flash. If it is possible to record one in a video, I surely have it!

It was during one of my late-night watch inspections, while panning the horizon that I spotted a huge bright glow coming from over the NW horizon. This glow was surely coming from a large fishing vessel that was all lit up, harvesting the sea. We are now just 600nm off the South American coast and converging with it. As always, when a vessel nears land, the hazards increase, and vigilance must increase to stay out of harm's way. The large fishing vessel over the horizon did not appear on my A.I.S., which is a bit concerning. I can only hope he has an A.I.S. receiver on board and is receiving my signal. The receiver is much cheaper to purchase than the transmitter.

DAY 197

Sailors Run is now hauling ass in the SE Trades! Yahoo! Debbie is waiting for me in Bahía and has fresh salt-free water that she will bring out to me once I'm across the finish line. It is possible that, when I arrive, I might miss the high tide necessary to get across the bar and might have to anchor in the open roadstead anchorage off-shore overnight.

I would like to share with you one of the hardest things about a voyage solo around the world unassisted south of the 5-great capes. In my mind, the most important thing is remaining confident in your abilities to pull it all off. I must admit this is very difficult when you and your small vessel are in perilous seas and winds thousands of miles from the nearest help. This is further exacerbated when it goes on over a duration of 4.5 months that is filled with numerous gales and storms. This scenario is a huge grinder, chafing away at your personal mettle, something far greater than one can even imagine.

The confidence that is required comes from the knowledge and experience about sailing in heavy weather conditions that you bring, as well as knowing you are on a strong and well-designed boat. That confidence is shored up and supported by the beliefs of friends and family that you can do it.

Let me give you a couple of examples. Debbie is my greatest supporter and continually tells me and others that I am the best sailor she knows, and I can do this voyage. Another example is like this: I was completing my first rounding of Cape Horn in 2009 and sailing up the Rio De Plata River, a shallow 200-nm body of water approaching Buenos Aires, Argentina. I was exhausted and wanted to make the marina at Yacht Club Argentino before dark. I started up my Perkins diesel and motor sailed a knot faster than I could go without the motor. It was after only two minutes the engine seized and was a total loss. I hadn't checked the oil, as I knew it was full, but because of a knockdown in a storm and a broken dip-stick tube, all the oil was outside the engine in the drip pan.

I'm not a wealthy person by any stretch of the imagination, and this engine scenario was going to cost me $13,000 dollars. Debbie was excited to celebrate the successful Cape Horn trip with me in Buenos Aires. All of these events had shattered my confidence. I was seriously thinking about running the boat up on the beach and walking away. I ended up pulling my emails that evening, and there was this one brief email from my friend Willy. He seemed to know right where my mind was, and he wrote this, "Jeff, you have successfully rounded the greatest cape of all, Cape Horn, and you are nearly there. Now, just kick its F*n ass and sail that boat right into Yacht Club Argentino and grab onto something!" You cannot imagine how that shored up my confidence. Suddenly, everything became perfectly clear, and it was obvious what I had to do.

So, I just want to say thanks to all of those who have encouraged me and shored up my confidence, helping to make this voyage a success. I do believe we all get by with a little help from our friends.

DAY 198

Trade winds continue to build, and today, Sailors Run is close reaching once again, on course and with good speed.

I became alarmed when 22 targets suddenly appeared on the A.I.S. Once I pulled up the target list, I saw they were all over 600 miles away. It seems there was some sort of atmospheric conduit that had opened up the propagation for me to be able to receive these signals from so far away. After about 15 minutes, they disappeared off the A.I.S., and everything was back to normal.

The Jefe'

Still no rain, and I'm making coffee with the much too salty water, just trying to weather through this drought for a few more days. I have not yet resorted to drinking my urine. My daughter Ginger, thoughtful like she is, suggested I serve it in a nice tea cup, add some herbs, and sip it like an exotic tea. I'm sure most exotic teas have a name, and possibly, this one should be called Me-Tea! What do you think, mates?

Slipping along, thinking about sipping it up, the Jefe'.

DAY 199

Today, we find ourselves sailing along in slightly lighter winds that forecasts say will drop even more in the next two days.

At last, today, I caught a small 24-inch Dorado. It weighed in at approximately 4 lbs. I cooked it, and it will be enough for two dinners. Yea, fresh food once again from the sea!

It was later in the afternoon as the winds were moderating that I went forward to slide the block aft on Patches, so I could let her all the way out to gain speed. I grabbed hold of my forward lower shroud on the lee-side of the mizzenmast as a hand-hold and felt it start popping strands as it became very loose in my hand. I scrambled back to the cockpit, dropping the mizzen sail to unload the mast. Then, I took the halyard forward to the hawser hole amidships on the leeward side where I attached it and tensioned it to help stabilize the mast. It was then that I thought, had the forward lower shroud on the windward side let go, it would have popped right off, and most likely, the deck mounted mizzenmast would have toppled into the sea.

I made a monkey's fist of sorts and tossed a string over both spreaders on the mizzenmast. I used this to pull a line up over them, around the mast, and then I tied a long bowline knot into it, which I used to secure it to a deck cleat on the port side, giving the mast some much-needed support. This enabled me to retrieve my one and only halyard on that mast. Now I could pull a set of blocks aloft to hoist myself up the

mast and replace the unraveling shroud with a piece of 7/16"
line. This project would have to wait until daylight, as it was
already getting dark.

During the night, on one of my checks topside, I saw a
small poorly-lit fishing boat pass within 1-2 nm of me.

DAY 200

I began my day at 5 a.m., anxious to make the mizzen opera-
tional once again. The breeze was up, and we were close
reaching at 7 knots in 6-8 ft. seas. I hoisted the blocks aloft on
the halyard and attached the bosun's chair to the end of them.
As I was climbing into that chair, many things were running
through my mind, like we are going pretty fast; maybe this
could wait, and if one of those shrouds that are only 5 years
old has failed, what about the other five that my life is now going to have to depend on? I wondered what it might be like to
ride the mizzenmast into the sea, and I was unable to visualize
a good way to do it. Oh well, at least, I had my inflatable life
jacket on as a safety harness.

I began pulling myself aloft with my go-pro camera
strapped on my head to record the event. Fortunately, I didn't
have to go up over 25 ft., but even at that, there were a couple
of times that I came loose from the mast. This sent me flying
out and slamming into the shrouds that were trying to slice
and dice me, then back head-on into the mast. During one of
the impacts, the camera took a bite out of the skin from the
bridge of my nose.

Once I was at the spreaders, I could see that only three of
the 19 strands were still holding the shroud aloft. I quickly inspected the other three terminations at the spreaders, and they
seemed to be golden. I hope they will stay that way for the remainder of this voyage. It was easy to pop off those final 3
strands, and I tossed the shroud clear of the boat and into the
sea. It streamed alongside the boat as it was still attached to the
chain plate below. I pushed the stem-ball fitting up out of the

spreader position and replaced it with the 7/16" line. I tied a figure eight jam-knot into the end and sucked it down onto the cup of the hole it passed through. Once on deck, I rigged up a small set of blocks and tensioned the line, so I could remove the long bowline knot and clear the sail track for the mizzen sail to go back up. Soon, the sail was up, and we were powered up once again.

I believe the rigging on the mizzen is a substandard wire, at least not 316 stainless, as it shows signs of some rusting. I will replace all the shrouds on this mast before putting to sea again.

DAY 201

Still sailing along nicely and just received an email from a friend saying, in the early morning hours, Ecuador had another 6.8 earthquake. I was anxious to hear if Debbie was all right, and later, I received an email from her reassuring me she was. The earthquake occurred as she was sleeping in her tent under the eaves of the house, and she awoke to the screams of a neighbor as the quake began. Debbie bolted from her tent, getting clear of the house, and ran down into the garden area, where our friends Dan and Amparo were also getting out of their tent. Debbie said nothing too much really happened, as the earthquake was deep in the ground, and no tsunami warning was issued. Also, the military started immediate patrols of the area to check on things and keep the peace.

It was later in the day when Debbie was at Puerto Amistad at the marina office that another tremor was felt. They all rushed out of the office to the middle of the street. She said the girls from Amistad were all frightened and crying as they hugged each other. Pilar, the head of the office, received a phone call that her father had fallen, hit his head, and wasn't breathing. Debbie and Pilar went with the new owner of Puerto Amistad, who is a doctor, and raced about 30 minutes to where her father lived. When they arrived, other family members were there, but Pilar's father lay dead upon his bed. Our thoughts and prayers go out to Pilar and her family. Sometimes, we fail to remember just how fragile life is.

I'm hoping to arrive at the finish line on Friday and must get there by 2:30p.m. to be taken in across the bar. It is going to be very close as to whether I make it in time.

I received more information on salty water yesterday from a former California water district employee, who is also a friend and sailor. He said one of their wells was putting out water at 1100 parts per-million salt, and they considered that potable, although their customers complained about the salty taste. He says they believe you can drink water up to 2000 parts per million without harming your body, although it would taste salty. My current water supply is down to three quarts, so I should be good through Sunday. I damn well better be there by then, the Lord willing.

Last night, I saw eight ships pass during the night; the closest one was within 3 miles.

On watch, preparing for shoring-up!

DAY 202

Today, I find myself sailing in frustratingly light winds, attempting to get to the finish line to *seal the deal*. I flew the spinnaker for 5 hours until the winds became too fickle to keep it up.

I was amazed at the amount of shipping traffic I found Sailors Run in while sailing across the Gulf of Guayaquil. I had 20 targets on the A.I.S. all at once. At one point, I thought we were going to become peanut butter when we found ourselves sandwiched between 3 ships, all within 4 miles of each other and going in different directions.

As night closed in on us, the vessel traffic seemed to disappear, and 30 miles off-shore, there appeared to be no fisherman. With the guard alarm that goes off if any ship approaches within 7 miles, at last, I was able to catch a little sleep here and there.

DAY 203

I hope today will be the day we close the deal and arrive in Bahía. I'm starting to feel very emotional as I look forward and watch Patches as she pulls along, brandishing all her scars from the voyage. Behind me, the Monitor Wind Vane chatters along as the pendulum shaft bounces up and down loosely in its framework, yet still continues to get the job done after all these thousands of miles.

The voyage suddenly seems so real and nearly complete, a voyage that might be remembered long after I'm gone.

This last night became a nightmare, as I noticed what looked like very bright stars low on the horizon, many of which were twinkling what seemed like way too much. Soon, I was sailing into one of the largest bunch of fishing pangas, 24-foot open boats, and this was not a pleasant experience at all!

Here I was, dog-assed tired and desperately trying to cover ground towards the finish, and I find myself confronted by the largest concentration of boats and nets I have ever seen. They had more than 30 nets stretched out before me, and my encounter with these fishing crews of four to six crew members in each panga amounted to a lot of yelling back and forth as I neared their nets. They, of course, were not aware that Sailors Run can sail right over a net as there are no appendages under the boat that can snag the net. A couple of times, I was able to sail around the nets, but to do so, I had to go through some pretty fancy maneuvers, while the fishermen were shining lights in my face and attempting to stay between me and the net. I tried to cooperate with them, but when it meant going back the way I had come, that was the final straw. With lots of screaming and yelling from them and nearly colliding with the panga, I sailed directly over their net. When the net popped up clear of the stern of Sailors Run, they suddenly became very quiet.

My main problem was, at each net, I had to go through the same process. On one such occasion, I was skirting out around the strobe light that was located on the very end of the net, when here comes a panga with an exceptionally loud crew defending the net. The skipper of this panga was intent on blinding me with his million-candle-power spotlight, a most discourteous thing to do, but after all, there are five of them and one of me. I finally had just about enough of this crap and grabbed my million-candle-power light and shined it in his face at very close range. It was amazing; suddenly, he shut his light off, then so did I. After several minutes had passed, with them staying between me and their net, he suddenly shined the freaking light in my face again. Of course, I blasted him right back, and once again, he turned his light off.

At last, I sailed clear of the end of the net, and just as the panga began to speed off, the skipper hit me once again in the face with the hellish beam from his light then shut it off before I could return the favor. I'm pretty sure he went away figuring he had bested me in the flashlight war! Oh well, such is life on the high seas. I believe I was called some very bad names during these encounters; after all, I was the outsider. As I sailed clear of all the nets, I felt pretty much unwanted by my fellow seamen.

Needless to say, by the next day, I was becoming extremely exhausted and still had not made it to Bahía.

THE FINAL HOURS OF THE VOYAGE

Today, with just 40 miles to go, I find myself in light air and up against a time deadline. I'll have to hustle to have any chance of catching the high tide required to get across the bar into Bahía. After being at the helm all night, I decided to continue steering by hand to get as much speed as possible out of the light winds.

In the end, it was not meant to be. I missed the tide by about 30 minutes. I crossed the finish/start line after 203 days,

8 hours and 49 minutes, having traveled about 25,147 nautical miles to make it back. However, none of this stopped Debbie from getting a panga and bringing me not only one of the greatest hugs and kisses I have ever had, but she also had fried chicken, fries, and rum. There were also some very much-needed gallons of fresh, clean drinking water. This all made a nice ending to a colossal voyage. Yet another night just short of the safety of a protected harbor but very much different from all those other nights, as this one would not be spent alone.

Tomorrow, late in the afternoon, I will cross the bar. Then life can become a little less spontaneous and wild, a change that I'm sure will feel just fine, at least for a little while.

I send a special thanks to all of my followers who have been riding along. I want them to know how much I appreciated all of their emails and the great support they have given me.

The Jefe'.

Current Stats

Position
Bahia, Ecuador.

Distance
Miles sailed last two days = 223 NM
Total miles sailed so far = 25,147 NM
Miles left to go to finish = 0 NM

Days 181-203

Sailors Run looking a little grungy after 203+ days at sea.

My last 5 gallons of water, containing nearly 2000 PPM of salt.

Land Hoe in Bahia!

May 2016 and I'm one happy dude to be in off the "Big Blue".

Debbie to the rescue after I crossed the finish line of Bahia.

A successful voyage behind me. Now, Debbie and I can celebrate.

A perfect cake for the Celebration.

Chapter 14: Afterthoughts on the Voyage

There are many things that come to one's mind after such an achievement, like: *what could be next?* First, let me try to wrap my head around what has just happened. So far, no matter how hard I try, the immensity of what has happened is still mindboggling to say the least. One shall never fully understand such an adventure until you take on a challenge so large, covering such an enormous space of time, where you must deal with countless hardships that are life-threatening. Yes, and it must be done alone, far from any help in what can only be described as a war zone.

The duration of the voyage was extended by at least 30 days due to major failures. What were the major events that, over a period of time, pushed me dreadfully close to failure?

1. The genoa that was only five years old had serious sun degradation, whereby it ended up with no less than 50 repairs and patches. This caused me to use it far less than I normally would, hindering my ability to cover the great distance I needed to travel quickly. This problem arose within the first week of the voyage.

2. The failure of the main boom gooseneck that had just been re-manufactured in Mazatlan, Mexico just months before the journey began. This failure happened about 6,000 nm into the voyage and was a hindrance over the remaining 19,000 miles. This failure only allowed me to fly the main with one reef in it and made the sail far less effective when going to weather.

Now, with days added to the journey, my problems started to domino, and the effects of these situations ultimately put the entire voyage in jeopardy of failure. With the additional days added, food supplies that would have been more than adequate were called into question.

The supply of water, always a top priority, became life-threatening when not one but two water makers failed along the way. I was forced to drink water with nearly 2000-parts per million of salt and crossed the finish line with only three liters of brackish water left on board. I must admit it was a horrible experience to live each day of those last few weeks with this salty taste in my mouth, and it seemed to get worse by the day. I could only guess at the harm this excess salt permeating throughout my body might be doing to me.

The number of things that failed and went wrong during this voyage seemed amazing to me, as well as the number of friends and family that followed along. I believe it is important to make that list available for anyone that might think of doing something this challenging on their own.

FAILURES

Wind Generator - Failed on the first day out and never would produce power thereafter.

Genoa - Started going bad in the first week after never having a problem with it up to that point.

Lines - Some new sheet lines and reef lines in the boom that were purchased from a marine chandlery in San Francisco started chafing through due to inferior quality. Where do they get this shit?

Steering Cables - Although these cables were replaced right before the voyage, they failed twice. The thing to be aware of here is, the Southern Ocean is ferocious and will find any weak links that exist in your equipment.

Refrigeration – Failed, and one should never be solely reliant on any one system, especially for your nutritional needs. I think about dehydrated food: it's light and takes up little space yet totally useless without adequate fresh water. For me, the failure of the refrigeration offset the failure of the wind generation as less power was needed.

Afterthoughts on the Voyage

Wind Vane - The three times that the breakaway tube on the Monitor wind vane broke is just one reason you need to be MacGyver with lots of spare parts. The wind vane is no doubt the most valuable asset to the single hander, as it is simple, non-electric, and runs energy free while still doing the work of three able-bodied seamen. It can steer the boat under most conditions.

Gooseneck - The main boom gooseneck is one of those pieces of gear that is not easily repaired at sea, nor would you expect having to fix it. It is also a piece of gear that must be respected. For me, the risks involved in a jury rig were just not worth it!

Fire - The electrical fire that filled the cabin with smoke is something that could happen on any vessel at any time. This particular problem occurred at night, and thank God, I was sleeping lightly and woke up to the acrid smell of burning insulation. In hindsight, a smoke and carbon monoxide detector could be very helpful in waking you up in this extremely dangerous situation.

Propane Line - The line that supplied propane to the cooking stove and operated flawlessly for 35 years suddenly broke with the excessive heeling and violent motion of the Southern Ocean. Only by sheer luck and a good sense of smell was the impending disaster that could have occurred thwarted. Always expect the unexpected.

Watermaker - The failure of my otherwise flawless watermaker that, after 16 years of faithful service, quit is something that must be anticipated and is a real possibility with less than new equipment.

Backup Watermaker - The second water maker that failed, a hand operated one, was simply an oversight by me. It was plainly noted on the device that it should be serviced each year, a hardly likely occurrence when out cruising. A 5-year cycle is more realistic and possibly adequate.

Autopilot - The loss of my electronic autopilot, a very reliable unit, was once again the power of salt water being forced into places it never normally encroaches. This loss was huge, as it was one of the devices that kept me free from having to stand at the helm 24/7. Not only that, it is the best way to steer the boat in winds of under 7 knots. It also can steer the boat if the cable steering fails, a really big concern, since it happened twice along the way, and the second time, there was no autopilot.

Radar - The loss of the radar was huge for many reasons. It was over 17 years old, and the silicone seal around the keypad was cracked due to age. Once again, the Southern Ocean discovered this weakness and injected salt water into the electronics, wiping it out. Granted, I had AIS that told me where ships were and let them know where I was, but other obstructions, like less-sophisticated vessels, such as South American fishing boats, icebergs, islands, and debris, are not part of that system. Neither are Coast Guard or military vessel for obvious reasons. My point is that AIS is no substitute for radar!

Block - My mainsheet double block that exploded is a pretty normal thing that might happen or any block for that matter, as they will surely be tested if you dare venture into the realm of the Southern Ocean.

Rigging - The rigging on the mizzenmast, where one lower shroud failed, could have meant the loss of the entire mast. Had the strain been on the side that failed, the mast wouldn't have stood a chance. This rigging was only 5 years old, and you would think adequate for the trip. These days, one must be sure of the quality of what we purchase, especially when it comes to replacing such important equipment. Our lives might depend on it.

I can only say this list is just the major items that went to shit. In total, I used 13 rolls of electrical tape, mousing wire, and God knows the amount of patch material, thread, silicone, and anything else that had adhesive power. There are never enough spares to feel totally at ease.

In a nonstop circumnavigation, where you are going to travel the distance that most hearty world cruisers would normally travel if cruising full-time in five years, and you set out to do that in just 6 months—think about it!

My final thoughts on this adventure are that, for those that might follow in the Jefe''s wake, just remember this was a voyage of passion, and I did it realizing it could not only cost me my boat but also my life.

So real, your amigo, the Jefe'.

Acknowledgements

First, once again, I must thank my loving wife Debbie for allowing me to risk our home and my life to partake in the greatest adventure of my life.

I must also thank my family members for supporting me and having understanding about the sometimes-crazy things I do.

I owe Sarah Wescott tons for all the time she put in doing the first edit of this book. She truly helped me get my ideas out of my head and onto the pages of this book. Sarah is an experienced sailor with many miles under her keel and a dear cruising friend. Thank you so very much, Sarah.

Additional editing was done by Bruce Powell, a long-time cruising friend, who read and reread the book so many times I'm sure he committed the whole thing to memory. He also provided many great ideas. Thanks, Bruce.

I must thank my son Daniel, an avid sailor, for his efforts to bring all the loose ends of this book together and get it put into publishable form. Thanks, Dan.

I also want to thank Bob Perry for designing the Baba-40 and making it so strong. I have never doubted the boat at any time in all my travels aboard Sailors Run.

About the Author

Jeff Hartjoy spent his early years pretty much unaware of the sea and sailing. It was not until, at age 22, when his schoolmate Dan Kelly invited him to Lake Couer d' Alene Idaho to go sailing that a passion was unlocked, and he never looked back.

When Jeff was 12 years old, he asked his mother, if you could do whatever you wanted in the world, what would you do? After several minutes of thought, she said, "Travel the world, see the beautiful places, and experience the different cultures." After hearing this, Jeff knew in his heart that he too wanted to live his mother's dream. It wasn't until Dan Kelly introduced Jeff to sailing and the free energy (wind) that Jeff could see a way to realize his dream of traveling the world under Sail.

In 1999, Jeff quit his job at the power company and took off with his wife Debbie. The two of them spent the next 17 years living their dream and sailing 85,000 miles together.

Currently, Jeff is taking on more solo adventures, as Debbie wants to spend time with grandchildren and be a part of their lives. Debbie, as of yet, has been unable to drag Jeff from the sea and his passion for sailing.

Endnotes

[i] Jefe': Author Jeffrey Hartjoy's nickname, Spanish for "the boss" and pronounced "heff-ay."

[ii] Five great capes: Cape Horn (South America), the Cape of Good Hope (Africa), Cape Leeuwin (Australia), South East Cape (Australia), and South West Cape (New Zealand).

[iii] Gooseneck: the critical hinge that connects the boom to the mast.

[iv] Brightwork: the lunatic practice of covering perfectly good teak with varnish.

[v] A.I.S.: Automatic Identification System. An AIS-equipped system on board a ship presents the bearing and distance of nearby vessels in a radar-like display format.

[vi] Zarpe: exit papers when leaving a country by boat, which would normally indicate the next destination. In this case, the boat was leaving Ecuador, and the next destination was…Ecuador, which caused some consternation.

[vii] Panga: A type of simple motor-boat popular with fishermen in Mexico and Central America.

[viii] Furler: Roller Furling System, whereby the jib or headsail is rolled up around the forestay in order to furl it (reduce its size) to make the sail more manageable in higher winds.

[ix] Hove-to: phrasal form of "heave-to": to bring a boat or ship to a near stop by steering into the wind and leaving the jib or headsail backed to windward. It results in a slow, steady, and relatively comfortable ride on a sailboat at a near standstill.

[x] NM: nautical miles, equivalent to 1 minute of latitude, or 1.15 statute miles, or 1.85 kilometers.

[xi] Spot locator: a portable satellite device that can report position and transmit a distress signal from most of the world's oceans. See www.findmespot.com

[xii] Drogue: a device towed behind a boat to slow it down to lessen the risk of capsizing or pitch-poling in extreme weather.

[xiii] Man-overboard-pole: a piece of equipment to help the skipper find a crewmember that has fallen overboard. Completely useless when single-handing.

[xiv] Heaving-to: see note 9.

[xv] Sail-mail: a method of sending and receiving email over very long distances (thousands of miles) using the Single Sideband Radio on board a boat. See sailmail.com.

Made in the USA
San Bernardino, CA
12 September 2018